Social Media Marketing 2019:

Your Step-by-Step Guide to Social Media Marketing Strategies on How to Gain a Massive Following on Facebook, Instagram, YouTube and Twitter to Boost your Business in 2019

Gavin Turner

techniques outlined in this book.

By reading this document, the reader agrees that under no circumstances is the author responsible for any losses, direct or indirect, which are incurred as a result of the use of the information contained within this document, including, but not limited to, —errors, omissions, or inaccuracies.

Table of Contents

References

Introduction:

The number of people spending time on the Internet has grown to 4.4 billion based on statistics collected at the beginning of 2019. In addition to this number of Internet users, there has also been an increase in the number of active social media users. This study also showed that there had been a 9% increase in active social media users in 2019 - translating to over 3.5 billion users. These statistics are revisited every year in order to understand the trend in the number of Internet users, and how they relate to the increase in social media activities. In correlating the figures, one can quickly point out that there is a positive correlation between the two, as more Internet users are active on social media platforms.

With the numbers derived from the study of the growth on the Internet and social media users, there is a vast potential for businesses to tap into and reach out to more people. The Internet is vast and has a high potential for both small- and large-scale companies to help them grow, primarily through using the various social media platforms available.

However, just creating an account on a social media platform and simply posting product images once a week will in no way guarantee business success online. Many small and large businesses fail in their social media marketing campaigns as they struggle in finding and applying the right methods. It is just wasted time and effort to create accounts on these platforms without posting strategic and quality content, and expect that it would translate to business success.

For your social media marketing efforts to work effectively, you would need to have a deeper recognition of the various social media platforms and the different ways to correctly engage with your target audiences on these platforms. With this book, you will learn the best ways on how to influence your customers - from brand awareness to client engagement to making a sale and then maintain continued business growth on social media. This book consists of chapters that will provide you with the best strategies to reach your targeted audience on platforms like Facebook, Instagram, and Twitter. You will be well equipped with information and the right steps to take that would ensure a productive social media marketing campaign for your business.

The information and strategies presented in this book are based on my years of working as a Social Media Marketing professional. I have been able to help different kinds of businesses achieve their goals through the various social media marketing strategies outlined and have structured this book in a manner that would be of maximum benefit to you struggling with social media marketing. Each chapter ends with practical steps that you can apply to your business to actualize your social media marketing goals.

This book contains the essential steps you need to succeed in your social marketing campaigns, regardless of the type of business you own. It provides in-depth strategies that will help you achieve the following:

- Dramatically increase the sales of your products or services and boost target audience engagement by focusing on the social media platforms that your audience engages in.

- Increase brand awareness about your business to both new and existing clients for long term customer relationships and profits.

- Take your business to a global stage. With an effective social media campaign, you can reach out to more people regardless of their location.

- Reach out to your target audience better and avoid wasting precious time and money on people who may not be interested in your business.

- Market your brand and business effectively and efficiently across the major social media platforms.

The Internet has become accessible to more people as social media users keep increasing yearly. It is essential that you follow the latest marketing trends to avoid missing out on the numerous opportunities they offer. We cannot continue to do things the old way and expect to get new results. Many businesses struggle because of the inability to tap into this excellent opportunity that will help them reach out to millions of customers online to sell their products and services.

The strategies that you are about to read will help your business stay relevant and become successful in making sales through social media. So let us discover all about social media marketing and how it can benefit your business, beginning in the next chapter.

Chapter 1: Social Media Relevance in Today's Business

Chapter 1: Social Media Relevance in Today's Business

1.1 Social Media and Social Media Marketing

To the average online user, social media is an online platform where you meet new friends, read peoples' comments, and connect with old friends. However, there is more to it than just meeting new friends and reading comments. This chapter will not only open your eyes to the vast opportunities inherent in social media, especially when it involves marketing your brand and business, but you will also end up knowing more facts about it.

The term social media has a wide range of meaning to most people, depending on how they use the platform. However, in a broad and meaningful sense of its applications, social media is an online communication tool for sharing information in real time. It is a community-based platform where you can engage as many people who are willing to be a part of the discussion.

Social media marketing has become popular over the years, with brands taking advantage of the community-based platforms to market their services and products to a vast number of audiences. Social media marketing involves using marketing strategies to get people engaged with, discussing, and sharing the content about your brand or products in order to reach out to more people.

Social media marketing has proven to be an effective and efficient way for companies to promote their products or services on these popular platforms. The companies or brands make use of the various tools available on these platforms to promote their brands and merchandise in the most effective way possible. Each of these platforms is unique and different as marketers use different methods to improve their brands on these platforms.

When Did Social Media Start?

We have several social media platforms, and they have become a favorite means of online communication among internet users. Almost everybody who has access online is connected to one social media platform or another, and it has become an vital part of their lives.

The history of social media dates back to 1844 when Samuel Morse sent a message via telegraph from Washington, D.C. to Baltimore, Maryland. However, the first recognized social media platform, SixDegrees, was founded by Andrew Weinreich in 1997.

SixDegrees had over a million members on the platform, and it is regarded as the beginning of the social media revolution (Hendricks, 2013).

In the real definition of social media, we can regard Samuel Morse's telegraphic message as the first platform for social sharing. However, SixDegrees took social media to a whole new dimension and increased the number of members on the platform with whom you could share and make friends.

The early 2000s saw the emergence of more social media platforms like LinkedIn and MySpace, which quickly became popular. In 2004, the advent of Facebook changed social media activity when it took the world by storm with its user-friendly platform. Facebook started as a platform to share pictures and updates with friends and family and has grown even more by adding business features to the platform.

In the several months that followed, there was a wide range of social media platforms with different features. Twitter, which has developed into one of the most popular platforms with billions of users worldwide, emerged in 2010 along with other platforms.

If you check out the history of social media, you will notice that these platforms have been boosted with features that make it easy to communicate in real time.

How Social Media Marketing Differs from Traditional Marketing

Marketing has been an age-old method to boost sales and promote brands online. Marketing did not just start with social media, but it has improved with the ease of using these community-based platforms to reach out to more people.

The traditional way of marketing involves meeting and engaging with people physically or using channels like the telephone to talk to people. Before the advent of the internet, salespeople would frequently go door to door to promote one product or another. In addition to that, who hasn't received numerous calls from telemarketers trying to pitch their products through the telephone?

The above methods are the traditional ways of marketing products and services. They involve a form of physical engagement as the salesperson is in contact or proximity with or is directly speaking to, the potential clients.

With social media, marketing has taken a new dimension, since you can now reach out to millions of people in real time. Social media has made it comfortable to use fewer resources to reach out to more people and expand your horizons.

Let's look at how social media marketing differs from the traditional form of marketing:

1) Wide Range of Scope with Social Media Marketing

Social media platforms provide a more comprehensive range of audiences than the conventional method of marketing. The scope of social media marketing does not limit where you can reach, as you will be reaching out to a broader spectrum of people.

With social media marketing, you can increase your customer base. Your marketing range is not limited to your locality. You have the opportunity to make your products, brands, and services globally-known.

2) Targeted Audiences

With the traditional way of marketing, you have to approach potential customers, not knowing if they will be purchasing your services or products. However, with social media, it is much easier to target potential clients who you know have a good chance of being interested, thus increasing your chances of making sales.

It is easy to convince someone who needs or wants what you are offering, and this is the essence of social media marketing. You can quickly sort those who are interested in a particular topic based on the community system that social media operates on, and, ultimately, increase your sales and customer base.

3) No Need for Personal Contact

In traditional marketing, you have to be in contact with the person to be able to pitch your sales. Potential clients often find this irritating, especially when they are in a bad mood. With the traditional method of marketing, you cannot predict the mood of the client, so you have to take your chances. In addition, you need to possess fantastic communication skills to convince your clients and make sales.

The use of social media eliminates the need for one-on-one marketing. In some cases, the prospective buyer you are trying to persuade may not be in the right mood at that moment. However, the truth is, many people are in a relaxed mood when they are online, especially when on friendly social media platforms. Thus, they are in the correct frame of mind and are more likely to show interest in your product when they come across it online.

4) Advertise to More People at Once

With social media marketing, you can advertise to more people at a time, which saves time and resources. It is time-consuming to go from door to door or call one customer after another, saying the same thing over and over again.

Social media marketing eliminates a repetitive process since you can market to more people at the same time. Your post can reach out to hundreds or thousands of people without starting a discussion with each one personally. The use of social media in marketing saves time and energy, and you can reach more people with less effort.

5) Real-Time Marketing

The traditional method of marketing involves a long

process before the final rehearsed product is pitched out. This process requires an entire marketing agency with an art department, music department, and other departments to help start a marketing campaign.

With the speed of social media, the outcome is more of a real-time based process. The social media analyst will have to be ready to pitch content quickly to reach out to people online. The social media experts have to be able to produce content, images, and videos concerning trending topics to attract people online.

6) Use of Analytical Tools with Social Media Marketing

It is difficult to measure your success rate with traditional marketing since you cannot collate or obtain data effectively. Social media platforms have analytical tools that help regulate your success rate using various analytical tools that we have access to on these platforms.

You can measure your progress in marketing with these social platforms and analyze data to determine the best approach for your desired results. The analytical tools will help in improving your marketing strategy, and this is one significant advantage and difference in social media marketing compared to the traditional method of marketing.

7) Active Involvement on Social Media Platforms

People are busy on social media posting comments, and liking and sharing content they find interesting to their friends, families, and followers. There is two-way communication with social media platforms, and this ensures that your potential clients are actively involved when you market your brands and products.

The potential of increasing awareness and sales is high with the dynamic nature of social media platforms. Traditional marketing is more passive, which makes the job more difficult; it takes patience and enough convincing to get a client active in the discussion while you try to pitch your product.

8) Social Media Is Informal

Social media platforms give more room for expression than other mediums of marketing. Traditional marketing is more formal and less expressive and does not provide as much room for creativity.

Social media marketing requires that you be creative and more interactive to make an impact on these platforms. The potential clients are engaging on this platform, and you need to be quick in coming out with an appropriate response.

Social media has changed the manner with which we promote our products over the years. Most top brands now have a department or team dedicated solely to social media marketing since it has a high potential in increasing sales.

You cannot ignore these platforms if you are seeking to increase awareness of your brand through the internet.

Statistics on Social Media Platforms

The numbers on social media are quite astonishing as we have billions of active users on these platforms. As a business, these numbers mean a lot to generate leads and create awareness about your brands, and this is the essence of these platforms to business owners.

Statistics show that the number of active social media users has reached 3.48 billion in the year 2019. This shows a 9% increase in the number of active users since 2018, and the number is expected to grow exponentially.

Online marketers are very interested in such statistics and the major social media platforms with the highest number of users. Facebook tops the list, as the number of active users on this platform had risen to 2.32 billion by the time 2018 ended, according to Statista. Twitter is the next highest when it comes to competing with the number that Facebook pulls online.

Other popular platforms include Instagram, YouTube, and others with unique features that make them useful for marketing.

Social media has become so popular that half of the world's population is active on social media platforms.

Businesses are using these platforms to create awareness about their products while they interact with their customers. These platforms have become an essential tool for business owners to communicate with their clients. Customers are communicating directly with companies on social media platforms, and often have their inquiries answered within the hour. It is an excellent communication tool for businesses to pass information to their customers quickly.

With the vast number of active social media users, your presence on this platform will help you generate leads. You can easily reach out to millions of people on these platforms who will be interested in your products and services. With the way the social media platforms function, you can get in touch with these customers and build friendly relationships while you bring your products and services closer to these audiences.

Take advantage of this large population of users, and make money from your brands and products.

Case Study of Social Media Marketing

There are lots of social media platforms, and, as you know, each has its unique features. Social media marketing can help promote your business and new products to both existing and new clientele.

Over the years, we have seen a sharp rise in the number of companies with a dedicated social media team to promote their business. There has been an increase from 67% to 72% of companies using social media teams to boost sales on these platforms.

Dacia is an excellent example of a company that increased its leads and promotes its brand name through effective social media campaigns on Facebook. Dacia is a car brand located in Europe and is a subsidiary of the popular Renault cars. The company used a Facebook campaign to generate leads and improve brand awareness.

The results were phenomenal, and the company saw an increase in sales. The company placed Facebook ads on their latest products, which include the Sandero Stepway and Logan Stepway models. The Facebook platform has proven to be the perfect tool to generate leads and to run advertisements at reduced costs.

The result of the Facebook ads run by Dacia can be summarized in the following points:

- 45% reduction in cost by using Facebook leads compared with other forms of advertising.

- Record of increase in ads recalls by 27 points.

- Favorable increase in brand awareness and acceptance.

- Increase in sales of products displayed on Facebook ads.

Facebook ads can be tailored using various parameters, and this company made use of Facebook features to promote their products. They made use of pictures, videos, and images to advertise on Facebook to get their desired results.

This book gives a detailed guide on how to promote your business and increase sales through the use of popular social media platforms. With this understanding, you can generate ways to use these particular features to boost your brand name, increase leads, and boost sales through these platforms. The chapters of this guide book are presented in a simple way of giving information by accommodating the diverse ways through which readers learn effectively. Each chapter contains three sections structured to answer the questions of what, why, and how. The fourth and final section contains simple, quick action steps that you should follow to put all you have learned in that chapter to productive and practical use.

1.2 Why Social Media Marketing Is Important

for Businesses

Here are the reasons why social media marketing is right for your business.

- Social media platforms hold considerable potential to reach out to a large number of people. With over 2 billion active users on these platforms, you have to take advantage of the numbers these platforms pull.

- With social media, you can have access to people who have an interest in what you have to offer. You can also boost your potential to increase leads and sales when you focus on these targeted audiences. Businesses take advantage of the ability to target specific audiences.

- Companies can use social media platforms as useful tools for customer service. With social media, you will get real-time feeds, and you can respond faster to customers' queries on the platform. However, to achieve this, you have to be responsive to these platforms and keep your customers engaged.

- Social media also improves engagement with your brand, thus, increasing awareness. It would benefit you to learn how to use the features on these platforms to your advantage. You do not have to be formal using social media since you can get your customers engaged by using images, words, and videos.

- Social media platforms have significantly reduced the cost of advertising. In the past, companies had to pay exorbitant amounts of money to get their products advertised. With social media, your business can advertise and reach more people at a much more affordable cost.

- The existence of your company on social media platforms makes information about your company, brand, services, or products easily accessible. There has been an increase in people that are looking for brands on social media platforms. Your presence on social media works to your advantage. Ultimately, people searching for your brand on these platforms will have the right knowledge of your business.

1.3 How Social Media Marketing Works

Embarking on social media marketing is not always as easy as it may seem. We need to look at the steps involved in social media marketing.

1. The first thing we should do is assess our business and think of the best platforms that will suit the business. With the different social media platforms available, you have to set out plans on which platform has the best and most suitable features for marketing your business.

2. Choosing the appropriate social media platforms to promote your business is the next step. You should consider the popularity of the platform and how the features of the platform will be useful to your brand. There are several social media platforms available, and it would be an arduous task to effectively market your business on all of these platforms at once. You can choose two to three platforms to consistently promote your business online.

3. If you have the resources, get a team that can

manage your business on all the social media platforms available. If you cannot acquire those resources, you can choose the best platforms to promote your business.

4. Choose a brand name. Choosing the right brand name will most likely be the name of your business. Moreover, this will be the name that you will use on your handle or social media name.

5. Get a logo for your business that you can use on your social media account. If you don't already have a logo, you can get one for your business from a graphic designer.

6. Write an appropriate bio detailing your business profile on your social media platforms. It should explain what your business is about, and provide your website, addresses, and contact information.

7. Plan your posting schedules and what you will post. Plan the content, images, and videos that will help promote your brand.

8. Make use of the platform's paid advertising

campaigns to reach out to more targeted audiences.

9. Post regularly to engage your followers on these platforms.

Your Quick Start Action Step:

Before delving into social media marketing, you have to understand what social media marketing is all about.

We are going to give you some quick action steps to ensure that you succeed in starting your social media marketing business:

1. *Learn about social media marketing. There are some online courses where you can learn about social media marketing strategies. Some of the sites where you can learn about social media marketing are Alison.com and Udemy.com.*

2. *You can create free accounts on popular social media platforms like Facebook, Twitter, Instagram, and YouTube to start promoting your business.*

3. For a company with enough resources, you can employ the services of social media managers to help your business on various platforms. You can visit platforms like Freelancer, Fiverr, Upwork, and other online platforms that offer freelancing services to look for suitable freelancers who can help promote your business.

4. Engage your visitors regularly. Post informative and exciting content on a weekly, biweekly, or monthly basis. People love to read stories that keep them in suspense. Try to incorporate something that will attract the attention of your readers, so they will be always be looking forward to reading everything you have on your page.

5. Post videos that depict the benefits of your product or brand. For instance, if you are marketing a smartphone, you can decide to post a video of how the phone is used to track and recover a stolen car.

6. Post funny videos once in a while to attract people to your page. People will not hesitate to

visit your page once they know that they will see something that will make them laugh.

7. *Be prompt in responding to questions about your product or brand.*

Chapter 2:
Aligning Social Media with Your
Business Goals

Chapter 2: Aligning Social Media with Your Business Goals

2.1 Defining Your Business Goals

Once you have a basic understanding of the relevance of social media marketing to your business, the next step is to make sure you define your business goal and make use of social media to achieve this goal.

It is vital that you have a goal set and a plan on how to achieve that goal using social media marketing for your business. Without a purpose and a plan, you won't have direction, and your time spent marketing on social media will have no positive effect on your business.

More than half of social media users consider it as fun, while the few (including you) who see the platforms as an excellent opportunity to boost their marketing campaign can take advantage of the vast numbers of users and the ease of engagement on these platforms.

How are we going to align social media with our business? How are we going to take advantage of these friendly platforms to achieve our business goal?

These are some of the essential questions you should ask yourself when you want to start using these platforms for marketing. With these questions, you will be aligning yourself in the right direction to use these platforms successfully for marketing your business.

2.2 Business Aims and Objectives Using Social Media Marketing

We have to understand the importance of aligning business with social media marketing strategies.

Here are some aims and objectives to aligning your business with social media marketing:

- With social media marketing and the advancement of technology, you can easily reach out to more people.

- Social media marketing helps build confidence so you can compete with other industry players online.

- Businesses can avoid wasting resources on advertisements and campaigns that reach people who have no interest in your industry.

- You can reach out to even more target audiences as you increase sales and awareness.

- Create a channel that enables you to reach out

to your customers, and lets your customers reach out to you, as well.

- Social media marketing provides you with the opportunity to play on level ground with other brands or companies in the industry.

- Grow your brand and business globally with social media marketing; the Internet is nearly limitless.

- It enables you to reach out to a broader demographic of people, especially the younger generations that are very attached to the Internet.

- Take your business to the next level with social media marketing.

2.3 How to Align Business Goals with Social Media

The use of social media can boost your business within the shortest possible time; that is if you use it to your advantage. We've seen a lot of organizations get discouraged because their social media marketing efforts are not yielding any positive results.

In this section, you will be exposed to steps on how you can align your business goal with your social media campaigns for excellent results. You should follow the process below to achieve the best and most favorable outcome.

1. <u>Set a Business Goal for Your Social Media Marketing Campaigns</u> — The first step you have to take in order to blend your business goal with your social media marketing efforts is to set the right target. You do not have to be rigid with your marketing goals; be as flexible as possible. Setting up a goal for your marketing campaigns will require a thorough analysis of your business. What does your business need at this stage? Are you new in the industry and need to create more awareness? Do you need to drive sales or promote a new product? These are some of the questions you should ask yourself as you draw up a suitable goal for your social media campaigns.

   o If you seek to promote brand awareness, then you should avoid promotional posts or concentrate on any specific product. Instead, it would help if you are more content-based, giving information about your business in your campaign. Your campaign should generally be about the company, and the advantages and impact your brand is set to make.

- A company seeking to improve sales and leads should focus on promotional content and their specific benefits. Such campaigns should include more videos and images. Make use of the appropriate keywords to get to more targeted clients.

- You can also build a strong follower base for your brand through social media marketing. These are suitable for businesses looking to develop a strong customer base over the years as they engage customers more with a content-driven post.

- You can also set the goal of reducing the cost of advertising and promotion of your brand. You can set up the campaigns using social media to the budget of the company, thus spending less to promote your business effectively.

o Businesses can also set goals to provide responsive customer service to their customers. These goals are achievable with social media through real-time posting and engagement with clients on the platform. Building excellent customer service will boost your brand as the customers become more confident in your products and services.

2. Who Are Your Target Audiences? — You have to be aware of the people you intend to reach with your social media campaigns. These people must be interested in your brand, and you must devise a way of gaining their confidence. Research the categories of people that will be interested in your brand, products, or services. Finding these categories should be done before starting your campaign. It will be a waste of time and resources if your campaign targets the wrong audience. For example, you may sell women's clothing, but your campaign

data indicates that your marketing strategies are targeted towards men. No doubt, the aim of your social media marketing will be defeated. You can also target audiences in a particular location to boost sales and leads. This kind of campaign is specific to businesses that have physical stores in particular areas. Knowing that clients in these locations will likely find their way to the store, you can target such clients. Most social media platforms will allow you to adjust and plan your campaign, targeting a specific group of people. Depending on your type of business, you can change the age, gender, and demographics to match the types of people who will be interested in your industry. This is the reason why you need to research the audiences who will be involved in your business, so you can tailor your campaign to reach these audiences. Let's take a look at some of these social media platforms and the kind of people they attract:

- o Facebook, one of the most popular social media platforms, is suitable for any business. Facebook has grown from a family- and friend-based community to a business platform where you can reach out to all kinds of audiences. This platform provides you with the opportunity to tailor your advertisements to reach out to certain demographics, and other settings to reach out to specific people. This platform is suitable for any audience your business is seeking.

- Twitter is another popular platform with over a billion users of different categories. Twitter is easy to use but to achieve your goal of marketing, you need to have a vast understanding of its features and the kind of people on this social platform. You can find a wide range of audiences on this platform.

- YouTube is an online streaming platform to watch videos free online, and it has become instrumental in marketing products and services online. The platform can be used for educational, as well as entertainment, purposes. You can teach people how to use a product, or explain the brand to them with a video illustration. It is effective in promoting brands and services to your audiences in a more practical way.

o Instagram is a visual platform where you can post images and short videos for your audiences online. Instagram has grown rapidly with millions of active users since its launch, and many brands take advantage of this to show off their products and services. Instagram has become more popular over the years, it has mainly been used for posting images, but you can also post short videos.

3. <u>Analyzing Social Media Data to Help Your Business Grow</u> — If you intend to succeed with your social media marketing campaigns, you have to take an interest in the data driven by your campaign. However, businesses have to be

specific about the kind of analyses they want to study to ensure that they obtain the right data. Luckily for you, most of these social media platforms have analytical tools that can help you manage your data. With the analyzed data, you can establish some useful information to help you improve your campaign. With the number of likes, comments, and shares, you can determine how people are responding to your campaign. Also, with the data provided, you can determine the types of audiences that favor your brand, and you can tailor your campaign to target these people. You can specify the location of the people visiting your platform, the gender, and other data that can help you align your business to social media campaigns. There are also some third-party tools that you can use to analyze the data from these social media platforms. These third-party tools have various parameters that will improve your data explanation to get you your desired results. You can see which articles or posts generate more likes and engagement, and those that have less interest. With these analyses, you can determine which of these posts attract more positive reviews from customers, and which increase sales or leads. Then, you can tailor your other posts to what your audiences like and prefer. These analytical tools are essential in understanding how your campaign is performing, what you need to do to succeed in your campaign, and how to improve and increase engagement and leads.

4. Checking on the Competition — You have to have a well-planned budget to cover all the expenses of online social media marketing. One aspect you have to take into account is the amount you are able and willing to spend on paid advertisements. Facebook, Twitter, and Instagram all offer paid advertisement campaigns, which you can use to target specific audiences. These campaigns have been known to be very effective in achieving your goals and objectives in social media marketing. With the user data available on these platforms, you can use that information in your social media marketing campaign to send out specific advertisements to targeted audiences for a fee.

Facebook Ads is one of the best-paid advertisement campaigns; it is very flexible, and you can reach out to as many people as you need. The Facebook Ads campaign is very popular and effective because of its flexibility and the cost of running the campaign. You can plan the amount you spend on Facebook Ads to meet your budget plan and still expect a good result. However, you have to understand that the more you spend on Facebook Ads, the more people your ad campaign will reach. With an understanding of your target audience, you can pinpoint the number of people your ad campaign will target, as you set it to reach out to only those who will be interested in your business. Through Facebook Ads, you can choose to be more cost-effective; you can target only those people who will be interested in your brand, and ultimately spend less on ads. On the other hand, if you have enough money on your planned budget, you can spend as much as you need to reach out to more people. In essence, you can tailor your Facebook Ads campaign to your budget and still run an effective campaign.

5. <u>Quality Content Creation</u> — The next step in aligning your business to a social media marketing campaign is to create quality content. At this point, you must have an understanding of the best content that will move your brand forward. In creating an article, you must learn a balance in inputting images and videos in your post. Statistics have shown that posts with quality images and videos attract more attention, and this is a key to promoting the brand and increasing sales. When you make a post on Facebook or Twitter, accompanying this post with an image or video will get more engagement, and this will lead to sales. However, in posting content on social media, there are some things you need to take into consideration. Here are some factors that will make your content more appealing to a social media platform.

   o The material has to be relevant, and something your targeted audiences will find relatable. You do not want to be posting sport-related content in a niche that deals with household wares. It's irrelevant and will likely dissuade audiences from visiting your platform in the future.

- o It helps if you are flexible and more informal with your content. This is social media, and people like some fun when they are on these platforms. While driving down your point or making leads through a call to action, be flexible, and use an informal and friendly tone when addressing your followers on these platforms.

- o Make sure your article gets your targeted audiences to take some action on your platform. What is the point of using content to promote your brand if, in the end, you do not increase sales, leads, or the number of clients visiting your website? Place a call to action on your content by either promoting a product or promoting your platform with suitable links or forms to fill.

- o Use videos or images to boost

engagement with your content. Pictures and videos attract people and encourage them to read the content.

- o Get a content developer who can use the right keywords to increase ranking and get you more leads. Carry out keyword research to use the specific phrases that will boost your content and increase sales as the content reaches a more targeted audience.

- o Promote educational and informative content that readers will appreciate. Carry out proper research on the topic and create content that readers will find rich in information.

- o Use relevant link building in your content to boost its relevance online and increase your ranking.

- o One of the most critical aspects of creating content is the authenticity of the material. Ensure that your content and articles are original and authentic, and this will build trust in your brand.

Your Quick Start Action Step:

There is no time to waste in starting to use social media to boost your online campaigns. Here are some quick steps to begin:

1. *The first action is to set your business goal, and this will require an understanding of the present state of your business. You need to ask yourself what your business needs at present. Are you looking for ways to expand or grow your audience? Do you need to create more awareness about your brand? Do you need to promote a new product? The objective of your business will lead you to take the right steps and pursue the right direction to succeed in your business.*

2. *Choose relevant social media platforms to run your campaign. You can start with just a few of them, like Facebook, Twitter, and Instagram, which are all very popular. For instance, if your target audience is celebrities, you can consider platforms like Twitter and Instagram.*

3. *Registration is free on these platforms when*

you register with your proper brand name and logo.

4. Build a profile and bio that will tell users more about your brand.

5. Get attractive, business-oriented content on your platform, and make sure you regularly update your social media page with new material. Make sure the material is appealing and answers most of the biting questions that customers need to know about your product or brand.

6. Promote your product with organic content using the right keywords. For example, search for the word that is associated with your product or brand. For instance, if you sell laptops, try to incorporate keywords like "cheap", "affordable", "fast", "high-quality", "rugged" and "lasting battery" in your content.

7. Make use of paid advertisements to get your content across to audiences.

Chapter 3:
The Mindset Towards Becoming an Influencer in Your Industry with Social Media

Chapter 3: The Mindset Towards Becoming an Influencer in Your Industry with Social Media

3.1 What is Mindset?

Before we examine the mindset that is required to become an influencer on social media platforms, we have to understand what defines the word mindset.

Mindset is a general way of thinking or a broad point of view in any given matter. Your mindset will determine how you view a particular issue or a specific topic. Your mindset on an issue determines whether you see the point positively or negatively, and how you will react over the problem. Moreover, if you want to influence a particular subject, you must have a vast knowledge of the topic with a positive attitude towards it.

3.2 Importance of Mindset in Becoming an Influencer on Social Media

Now that we understand the meaning of mindset, how can mindset enable an individual to become an influencer on social media platforms? Here, we are introducing a new term, which is an influencer in social media marketing.

What do we understand from the word influencer? Moreover, how did it come into play in social media marketing?

A social media influencer is an individual that has access to a wide range of audiences, and can persuade them through their authenticity, reliability, uniqueness, and reach.

However, an influencer is not just related to social media marketing, and from all understanding, influencers have been around for a long time. To understand the world influencers in marketing, let's ask a critical question.

Have you ever bought a product or decided that a product is top quality when you see that the product being used is by a famous figure?

Most products record an increase in sales when they get endorsements from famous figures or celebrities. These are influencers who have convinced their followers to buy these products by endorsing such products either directly or indirectly.

These are excellent examples of influencers, and an influencer can also be someone who gets their followers, or a large number of people, to react to specific issues in a particular way. You will see companies using celebrities, top sports personalities, and politicians to promote their products to their followers, as it will give the products that much more exposure.

You can also become an influencer on social media platforms as you gain trust and confidence from your followers. Becoming an influencer will be immensely helpful to your marketing efforts and will make your social media marketing easier as you influence more people.

Becoming an influencer does not necessarily mean you have to be accessible as you can build from scratch and gain confidence from your followers. As a brand, you can become an influencer in your industry and share articles and posts to improve the lives of your followers.

So, how does mindset connect with influencing products or services to a group of people? Let's take a look at why mindset is vital in social media marketing.

Here are a few points about why mindset is crucial and helps you influence more people:

- You have to encourage a positive mindset about the product for you to push it forward to people. Believing in your brand is essential to have the zeal to promote the product to targeted audiences. This is because it is difficult to sell products or services that you do not believe in or don't have a passion for.
- There needs to be an understanding of the products and services, and what they can do so you can become a good influencer. Vast knowledge about the niche will help you speak favorably about the products. Research the products and the industry, and you can give an informed decision about the product. Learn more about the product and services, so with this broader understanding, you'll have the right mindset to talk to your followers.
- With a positive mindset, you will be willing to engage your audiences on issues relating to the brand or products. You are ready to do more

research to provide your audience with the right information.

- A positive mindset keeps you going on your social media marketing campaign and does not permit you to procrastinate on your activities on social media platforms. You will be eager to share your ideas and knowledge with your audience, who will also be anxious to learn from your interesting and informed posts. This approach will make you a trusted influencer in that area.

- If you are less interested in sharing anything that is not relevant to your audience, then you have the right mindset. You prefer quality over quantity, which your audience will appreciate over the competitors who believe in the opposite.

- Without the right mindset, you cannot stand the test of time in a particular niche, and you'll end up moving to a new business or niche. You'll tend to change brands and products because you do not hold the quality of a product in high regard and settle for any available product.

- Shift your mindset away from the idea that social media marketing is just another part of work. It becomes tiring, just like a duty one needs to perform. However, take it as a way to be around people you know and share happy topics that will benefit these people.
- Don't think that you have to be on every platform to make an impact. Just choose the one with which you are most familiar and use it effectively. For example, you could start by growing your influence on Facebook or Twitter first.
- In social media marketing, you should avoid having a mindset that leads you to look for ways to achieve fast results or cut corners. If you're going to become an influencer in social media, patience is required. You are not going to see a massive spike in sales immediately after you commence your marketing campaign; it takes time.
- Authenticity helps you earn trust from your audience; online users will see you as being real and genuine and not as someone who is trying to deceive them in getting their money.

3.3 How to Develop an Influencer Mindset

An influencer is someone who can dictate or manipulate how someone thinks or what they do. Influencers have become critical to businesses, especially since the inception of social media marketing. These influencers help the brand or business generate leads and promote sales and awareness.

You must understand that an influencer does not necessarily need to be social, but being sociable goes a long way to becoming an influencer in social media marketing. Good examples are celebrities and sports personalities; they may not have the time to be on social media platforms regularly, but they can get their followers to think a certain way with just a single post. A celebrity posting about a product is a form of endorsement, and it can create lots of positive hype about the product.

On the other hand, there are social people on these social media platforms with thousands of followers who are interested in what these people have to say online. These influential people can direct their followers, primarily when they endorse products or services.

You can become an influencer on social media platforms as you promote your business online. It is not that difficult, and in no time at all, you can become influential enough to get people to believe in your posts and articles.

Here we are going to show you what it will take to become an influencer on social media platforms. To become a social media influencer, you have to develop an influencer's mindset, and this will require the following steps:

1. Understand the Platform That Is Most Suitable for You — You need to realize that you cannot become an effective influencer on all social media platforms, so it is better to focus on one. To become an influencer, you have to choose the particular platform you are passionate about to work online. Passion is required, as this will push you to give your best and you will never get bored. Choosing one or two of the platforms to be very active on will require you to have a complete understanding of how those platforms operate. You should know how to use

the platform to generate buzz when needed. Twitter and Instagram are two of the most popular platforms with lots of users. With these platforms, you can quickly get your business across to thousands of people with just a post using the right keywords or tools, such as hashtags. With the consistent and regular posting of quality content on these platforms, you will become a top name in your specific industry. The kind of platform you will choose depends on the industry and what you intend to promote. If your niche requires more article-based content, then you should not hesitate to post your content on Twitter and Facebook. If you need to post more images and videos, then Instagram or Pinterest would be better platforms to showcase your products. Picking a particular social media platform will enable you to be focused and result-oriented.

2. <u>Develop a Passion for Researching and Sharing</u> — Influencers need to conduct rigorous research to present quality content for their followers. To become an influencer, you have to be ready to research related topics. The ability

to develop well-articulated and informative content is a much-needed skill for an influencer. You will also have to research what kind of articles would be suitable for your particular audience.

3. <u>Become an Expert in a Niche</u> — To gain your audience's trust, you have to be authoritative in whatever content you post. You cannot be an expert in all industries or niches. In promoting your brand or business, you have to create the impression that you are an authority in that niche. You will have to focus your attention and do more research on your chosen niche. For instance, posting pet-related content when you sell clothes is out of place; your targeted audience will not find such posts relevant to their needs. Develop the mindset to concentrate on a particular niche as you grow to become a trusted expert. Focusing on making posts for a different niche will only get your audience confused, and they may not end up following your brand on social media if your posts become too irrelevant to what they are searching for online.

4. <u>Think Outside of the Box</u> — Remember to be authentic and unique as you strive to be influential on social media. Readers love something unique and different, and you have to be different from others. You can follow people who are in the same niche as you on social media platforms but make sure to think outside of the box with your posts. Be creative with your posts as you get your users engaged with factual information. As you get creative, make sure that the content and posts you deliver are still accurate and educative. Do something that other influencers aren't, and in doing so, you will get amazing results. For example, you could provide content about the inner workforce in your organization. Make a compelling documentary on the people that are involved in the end product that the consumer gets, and how they work hard to ensure consumers are satisfied. You could also post a contest and reward the winners as a way of increasing engagement and awareness about your products and services. Be innovative in engaging your clients and give them incentives

in the form of a contest or prize.

5. <u>Develop a Strategy</u> — As a social media influencer, you need to have a feasible plan. With a well-organized plan, you will not divert from your project, and you will continue to provide quality content. As an influencer, to get to your audience, your content should be varied so it does not get too dull or predictable. Always keep your audience on the edge of their seats as you continue surprising them with your content. You should have a plan to post different kinds of content, such as informative content, personal content, descriptive product content, news updates on the industry, and others. This strategy will ensure that you keep your audience engaged and provide them with a wide range of informative, educational, and entertaining content. You can set a schedule of when to post particular kinds of content, and stick to it as you provide your audience with a wide variety.

6. <u>Post and Share Content</u> — You should understand that there is more to just posting

and sharing content on social media platforms. You have to understand the platform and when and how to post content to reach out to more clients. A platform like Twitter, which is more of a real-time feed, requires you to post when audiences are most active online. Yes, there are hours of the day when people are more productive, and there will be more views and engagement on your post. Research the peak periods on your relevant platforms, and when your targeted audience is most likely to be online. In real-time news feeds like Twitter, people are more interested in topics that are trending or occupying the top of the news feed. If people are very active on the platform, and your post has gone down the timeline, they might not see the post or react to it. However, if you post your content at the time when they are active online, it will appear as a real-time post on their news feed, and they will react to it on the platform. There are some platforms where your content will get more responses and reactions if it has a responsive image or video accompanying the material. Facebook and

Instagram are image and video-oriented platforms. For these platforms, you should make quality images or post an adequate video of high quality along with the content. Posting content with relevant tags or hashtags will get you more responses on these platforms. You have to understand how these tags and hashtags work to get the best use out of them when posting. Using hashtags that are related to the niche or post will help people easily find your content on these platforms when they do a search using those keywords or phrases. A fashion-related post using #femalejeans will be picked up quickly and appear on search results when people use 'female jeans' to search. You can use popular tags like #fashion as well, although it is likely to have been used by more people; the competition to get the top spot on the search list will be high. Taking advantage of this tagging will increase awareness and response on these platforms.

7. Create Time to Be Online — You have to be active on your favorite social media platform to become an influencer. You have to create time

and always plan your schedule to be online daily. There is no way you can be online all the time, but it is essential that you are active online at the right peak time. Plan your schedule to engage your audience at the right time, when the majority of them will be active on the platform. You will notice that influencers on your popular platform are online mainly when a hot, trending topic is being discussed. Don't miss out on these trending topics as you can engage more people when these topics are being discussed.

8. <u>Be Ready for Networking</u> — As an influencer, you have to grow your follower base, and you cannot achieve this by just expecting audiences to like your posts. You have to be ready to network as you build relationships with other influencers and bloggers, and share your posts across all other social media platforms. You can reach out to more people by connecting with other influencers and having them share your posts. You can build relationships where you share the influencers' posts, and they share your posts in return to expose each other to a

bigger audience. This action is common in circles of influencers as they build more traffic to their posts by helping each other out. You can also reach out to more people by blogging and sharing your posts with other bloggers. You can reach out to more people by networking with other bloggers; you can guest post on their blogs, and also have them share your link. Promoting your posts, especially with other influencers and platforms, is essential to reach out to more people. This approach will extend your reach, and people will trust you more as other influencers share your posts. Create a circle of trusted influencers across all platforms so you can extend your reach to a broader audience.

9. <u>Have a Consistent Mindset</u> — Be ready to be active and consistent as you keep your audience updated regularly. Social media is a very dynamic platform, and what is trending this hour may not be trending the next. Expect constant change and be ready to adapt to those changes. The longer you stay away, the more likely you are to be forgotten and replaced with

a new influencer. Be consistent and ensure that you do not leave room for others to take your spot on the level you have built up to as an influencer. Make sure that you are not absent for too long, so you stay relevant in the industry.

Your Quick Start Action Step:

Taking the right steps at the right time will help you achieve your social media marketing goals. To complete your objective at the right time, you should take the following steps:

1. *Take a week to analyze and understand your target audience and how best to approach them using the right platform.*
2. *Registering and building your profile on the appropriate platform will not take up much time.*
3. *The next few weeks should be used to create content on your platform, so the audience will be engaged when they visit your platform.*
4. *Remember, as you post your content, you should also share the content with friends and*

family and ask them to help you repost, retweet, or share.

5. *After a month of active posting of targeted content, you are now ready to dedicate time for promoting your platform. At this stage, you can engage other influencers and top bloggers for the promotion of your platform.*

6. *People are influenced by success stories and positive reviews by past users of your product. Try as much as possible to post the success story of your brand, and tell your users to visit your social media pages to leave positive comments about your brand or product.*

7. *Promoting your platform is a continuous process, but you can dedicate a month to active promotion to create awareness after filling up your platform with appropriate content.*

8. *Set a schedule to post at least three times weekly to attract new people. Engage with your audience about related issues and trending issues on the platform.*

9. *Keep posting and engaging as you follow your set schedule.*

Chapter 4: Finding and Serving Your Target Customers

Chapter 4: Finding and Serving Your Target Customers

4.1 Your Target Audience

Your social media campaigns will be a waste of time and resources if you do not get to the right people. If your goal was to promote your physical store online to increase the number of visitors, but all of your campaigns were directed to people outside your target group, then the objective of the social media campaign has been defeated as the aim was not achieved.

There are billions of active social media users, and there are all categories of people on these platforms. You have men and women of different ages and in different locations, and the trick of social media marketing is to meet those who are interested in your product or services.

Well, with the tools available on these platforms, this can be achieved; you can tweak your campaign to reach out to a particular set of people who will be interested in your product.

Facebook is one of the best platforms to carry out

targeted campaigns. With Facebook ads, you can easily edit your campaigns to reach out to specific and selected categories of people. When you are using Facebook ads, before posting the ads, you will be asked to choose the range of people that will see the advertisements or the set of people you want to target with the ads.

You can set the advertisement to reach out to people of a specific age, gender, and even location. With these settings, you can direct your ad to people who will be interested in the product or services.

However, before you start using Facebook ads, you need to do thorough research on the types of people who will be interested in your product or services. With this, you are increasing the chances of your social media campaigns being a success. There will be an increase in brand awareness, engagement, and sales, and this will increase profits in the long run.

In this chapter, we are going to focus on how to find your target audience to ensure that you do not waste time and resources.

4.2 How to Find Your Target Audience

In social media marketing, the target audience is the most crucial factor, and it is what makes social media marketing more relevant than other types of marketing. It is easier to reach out to the audience interested in your brand through social media marketing.

However, it takes an understanding of how to use these platforms to reach out to your audience. Otherwise, you will just be wasting resources. To ensure that we target the right people and avoid wasting resources with our campaign, the following steps are essential.

- Know Your Audience — In whatever you are promoting online, certain people will be interested in that offer. As one of our objectives with social media marketing is to target those people, we must first know these categories of audience. There is a direct relationship to the products or brands we are promoting, and the audience we are marketing to. In recognizing our audience, certain questions will arise. Are the products specific to men, women, or both? Where are the people interested in these products located? What is the age range of the people who are likely to be interested in the product and brand? Are the products geographically inclined to specific regions? These are some of the questions that have to be answered to understand the audience that will likely be interested in your products and services. By knowing how your potential audience relates to your products and services, you can determine the best people to target as customers.

- Evaluate the Size of Your Audience — There should be an estimate of the number of people that you want to target with a social media campaign. This type of data is essential to help plan and gather information about how well the campaign is going. With analytical tools that are available on your social media platforms, you can estimate the number of people your campaign will reach out to. A good example is when you make use of Facebook Ads while setting out the parameters to post the ads. You will be provided with an estimated number of people that the ad campaign will target. With this knowledge, you can now determine if the money to be spent on the campaign is worth the effort. You can also change the parameters to enable an increase in your targeted audience when using such tools. With this, you will know how to plan your campaign as you maximize your resources to reach out to more people. Facebook Ads are beneficial in analyzing the number of people your campaign is targeting. It can also help you make a plan as you improve on subsequent campaigns.

- Research Behavior of Your Audience — Knowledge is essential, and knowing how your target audience behaves will enable you to reach out to your audience efficiently and effectively. You can track the footprints of online users, and with this knowledge, learn about their behaviors. You can predict what they will do, so monitoring the audience will be easy. It is easy to track collective patterns and behaviors online; data can show you the websites they visit, and at what time of the day, and also how long they spend on these platforms. With this available information, you can also track the kinds of devices they use in their online activities. This information is very useful in learning about your audience and then formulating how best to reach out to these sets of people. You can provide video content if you find that your audience loves watching videos, or you can create podcasts for your audience. Others may like to spend time reading or going through specific blogs, especially those of your competitors. With this knowledge, you can expand your campaign to involve blog posting to get the attention of those who love reading. On platforms like Facebook, Twitter, and Instagram, you can check out which people your audience follows online to grasp an understanding of what will interest them. Check out your competitors to see who is following their social media accounts, and follow these people.

- In most cases, these people will follow you back without you asking. Thus, you increase the number of people following you and also raise awareness about your business. There are some tools, such as Google Forms and Survey Monkey, which can effectively provide you with data about the behavior of your target audience. This data is critical in analyzing the behavior of your audience to use for your marketing on these platforms.

- Attract Your Audience — The essence of knowing your audience and learning their behavior is to ensure that you can attract them. You know your audience, and you have managed to grasp an understanding of what they like. Now, you need to take measures to invite them to your platforms. Build and design a platform that will attract your targeted audience based on data analyzed on their behavior. Using the right images, avatars, bios, and display names will be based on your understanding of studying your customers. With that knowledge, you know what is expected when creating your profile. This step does not involve going after the customers, but having the customers search for and find you. It includes the customers coming across your profile and immediately understanding what it is about and following you. They quickly gained interest based on your bio, content, and images. All these have been put in place due to the analyses in the first step.

- Find and Connect with Your Customer — Now, the next step is to find and connect with your customers on these social media platforms, after creating your account and updating your profile. If you have an email list of your customers, you can easily connect with them by searching for them on the platform. Social media platforms allow you to search for people on your contacts by using their email address, so it will be easy to contact your existing customers, inform them of your new social media account, and build a following. Using Facebook Ads is another way of finding and targeting the audience on social media platforms. You can edit your Facebook Ads with certain parameters to target people that are interested in your business, and you can reach out to more people using this platform. With Facebook Ads, you can also input your email addresses to search for your contacts using these Facebook tools. However, there is another trick in using Facebook Ads to search for your contacts. You can input your email address contacts and create a lookalike audience to grow your following.

- With this lookalike audience, you can find and connect with more people on the platform who share similar interests with your contacts. Facebook can be regarded as one of the best platforms to promote your business. Facebook is often considered the best because of the high number of active users, and the tools that enable you to target an audience that has an interest in what you are offering. Another essential and simple trick in growing your audience with Facebook is to join groups of similar interests. Engage in the group conversation so you can become popular and promote your brand. Twitter may not be as popular as Facebook, but it is very influential for social media marketing. Just like Facebook, Twitter does have its own advertising tool, although it is not as flexible as that of Facebook. With Twitter Ads, you can search for people based on their locality, gender, and interests by using specific keywords, taking note of the people following them, and so on. Twitter may seem complicated at first, but if you can understand how to use the platform and follow people with similar interests, then you will benefit greatly. You can search for people by using the Twitter advanced search tool, and follow people to get noticed. People will likely follow you back, so you should search for people with similar interests. You can also gain a larger target audience when you search for your competitors; follow people who follow your competitors' platforms because they have similar interests to what you have to offer. Instagram is similar to Facebook as you can also filter your search and use paid advertisements to target audiences. While this platform is not as popular as Facebook and Twitter, it is growing in popularity, especially among young people and women. LinkedIn, as a business-based social media platform, is essential to meeting business people on a one-on-one basis. By creating a suitable profile of your business on LinkedIn, you give people with business prospects the ability to reach out to your business. As a business, you should encourage those holding important positions in your organization to create business profiles on LinkedIn. When people search within your niche using the right keyword, they can reach out to your business easily. Also, the target audience can reach out to your business profile as it will become an appropriate platform to provide customer services. You can take advantage of joining groups with similar interests to engage more people and grow your audience. Lastly, you can take advantage of popular platforms with massive follower bases by guest posting on these platforms. Guest posting is a common way to improve SEO content and build awareness about your brand. Guest posting is most suitable for new businesses while they seek to gain awareness and build an audience through an existing follower base. With guest posting, you can easily show that you have extensive knowledge in your particular field, and you can begin to build your brand as an authority in the industry.

The steps provided above are essential in building your connection with the target audience. Because it is important to target audiences that are specific to your business, you have to follow each step studiously to achieve your aims and objectives in social media marketing.

4.3 How to Connect with Your Target Audience

In the previous section, we extensively discussed how to find a target audience through social media marketing. With a clear understanding of the steps to take to find your audience, we can now move to the next level: connecting with the audience.

Social media marketing is a continuous process, and finalizing one step will lead to another. This section is one of the essential parts of this book, as there is an emphasis on the target audience and how to attract and connect with them. You might be able to identify the audiences that need your products or services, but without the right skills to communicate with these audiences, you could just be wasting your time.

How are we going to connect effectively with these target audiences and keep them attached to our social media platforms?

In this section, we will elaborate on the ways we can connect with these audiences that we have come to know and understand.

Here are some ways you can connect to more people on popular social media platforms:

1. Post Creative and Engaging Content — The kind of content on your platform determines how people connect with your business. Now that you know and understand the type of audience that is attracted to your business, you have to create suitable content that will capture their attention and enable them to connect more with you. Your viewers will determine the kind of platforms you use, and this will also determine the type of content. On Facebook, you can post images and videos, as well as text. You can post links to your websites or blogs, so, with Facebook, you can reach out to people with a variety of content.

2. On the other hand, if your audiences are more

inclined to images or videos, you can focus on social media platforms like Instagram and YouTube. Through all this, you must provide quality content to connect with your audience as they follow your platform and share your content. Since you know the type of audience that your business requires, research what they like to read about online, and check out what your competitors are doing to grow their following.

3.

4. <u>Be Consistent with Your Content</u> — Social media marketing is a full-time job, and if you cannot handle it alone, then employ a social media manager to carry out the responsibility of the task. If you want to connect with your audiences effectively, then you have to be consistent with the frequency of your posts on the platforms. In other words, your social media accounts have to be active as you post relevant content. Some social media managers have a posting schedule to stay consistent and connect with their customers. If you are absent

online for long periods, you might lose out on the connections you have made on the platform. The competition on these platforms is very high, so avoid creating a vacuum or being absent for too long, or your competition might take your spot. In a bid to stay relevant by posting consistently, post about topics that are relevant to your industry. Do not post just any mediocre content online; ensure that it is what your audiences will find engaging. Follow a schedule and a plan of what to post so that you can be consistent with your posting.

5. <u>Be Attentive to Your Audience</u> — You know your audience and understand what they desire, and now you can give them what they want in order to connect with them. In connecting with your audience, you have to be attentive and respond to your audience as fast as you can. Through the use of social media platforms, you can set your account to alert you whenever you are mentioned, whenever you are replied to, or whenever someone shares your content. You can use software like Google Alert, SocialMention, and Tweetbeep to give

you quick alerts whenever there are activities that concern you on your platforms so that you can respond as fast as possible. You may be required to pay a fee to use some of this software, but it is a good investment for your social media marketing campaign. You can also make use of the free features and notifications that are available on these social media platforms to respond to your customers. When you respond to your audiences as quickly as possible, you can keep your content active and build conversations with comments and replies. In so doing, you are connecting with other people as the content creates more buzz on the social media platform.

6. <u>Knowledgeable and Informed Responses to Your Audience</u> — You can connect with your customers and even more people when your replies and responses are knowledgeable. If you want to hire a social media manager, ensure that they have good knowledge about the business, or can carry out research as fast as possible and provide a good response on time. When the audience is aware of the ability

of your social media account to provide them with accurate and applicable responses, this builds trust in your brand. Trust is a very relevant factor in building a connection with your audience when marketing on social media. When your audience trusts that you are delivering quality and relevant content, they will share and retweet your content and let you connect with more people on the social media platform. If you want to connect with your audience, you have to be resourceful and take the time to research the content that you post on your account. Ideally, your content should be factual, informative, and entertaining.

7. Retweet and Share Content from Your Audience — You can connect with customers when you retweet and share their content. By doing so, you are building a personal relationship with your audience, as they will receive the notification that you have shared or retweeted their content. In most cases, people are happy to return the favor by sharing or retweeting your content to their followers, and thus, you can connect to more people online.

Sharing relevant content also gets you exposure; more people will get to see what you are sharing, especially if it is a trending topic. When sharing and retweeting content, ensure that the content you are sharing is relevant and of good quality. Share content from industry experts with your followers; you will be doing yourself a favor as they notice you and share your content, which will boost trust with your audiences. You can also comment on their posts and engage them in conversation. This could involve other people on the platform as you expand your connections and reach on the platform.

8. Social Media Platforms Build a Personal Connection — Customers feel more comfortable with businesses that have a personal touch and can reach out to their clients efficiently. As a business owner, you need to place your customers in high regard and create an avenue where they can easily reach you. Being accessible will build trust and confidence in your brand as you set up responsive customer service. With social media

platforms, you can get close to your customers and converse with them on a personal basis. You can chat with your customers individually using their first names and make them feel comfortable with your brand.

9. Moreover, you are keeping your customers satisfied as you take your marketing strategies to social media. Businesses have been using social media platforms as a suitable avenue to provide customer service to their customers. It is a more affordable and faster way of communicating with their customers as they seek to improve services.

10. Moreover, with these methods, you are making it less formal, and you help the customers feel more relaxed and comfortable while you promote your business. Here are some tips that can help you use social media platforms to attract and keep your customers:

11.

   ○ You do not have to be formal; give the customers room to express themselves freely, creating an atmosphere of trust.

- Be responsive and fast in replying to customers when they contact you, especially with questions or requests.
- Don't respond to your customers with prearranged templates; let your replies be as original and friendly as possible.
- Be active online and don't be absent when your customers need you.
- Be up-to-date with the latest events and happenings in your industry so you can give your readers informed replies.
- Be friendly with your customers; you can discuss something not business-related to keep them engaged and happy.
- Always create a pleasant and comfortable atmosphere when conversing with customers on these platforms.
- Be professional in your responses, and don't get too personal with the customers.
- Always try to check back with a customer you helped to know how the

customer is doing.

12. <u>Attractive Offers to Customers on Social Media</u> — With attractive offers, you can make your customers happy and get them engaged, as well as attract new customers on social media platforms. One way you can achieve this is to ensure that your social media followers enjoy free offers. You can create awareness on these platforms when you offer great gifts or deals. Most businesses share free offers to their followers on social media platforms before others even find out about those offers. Moreover, this creates lots of engagement on their platforms as customers keep up with the updates on the business's social media platforms; they want to ensure that they do not miss out on these offers.

13. An excellent example of this is if your business offers its customers a 'buy two products, get one free' deal. Some businesses share codes or vouchers on their platform that cut down on prices, or occasionally provide their customers with free products. Your platform will be

flooded with new and returning customers as they take advantage of the offers you provide.

14.

15. Redirect Your Followers to Your Website or Blog — If you want to convert your visitors on social media, then you should direct them to your blog or website. This technique is a unique way of keeping your customers and attracting new customers. On social media, your visitors do not get the complete view of your business, only a glimpse of what you have to offer. With every post on your social media platform, drop a link that directs your visitors to your website or blog, and encourage them to sign up for regular updates. You usually can't provide all the necessary information on social media platforms as you are mostly limited to words and content. It is best if you direct them to your blog or website so they can get an extended version of the content. From the website or blog, you can also get more information about the business, so direct your contacts on these social platforms to your site. A good strategy is

to have your website linked to your bio, so those who want to know more about you can go through your bio.

16. Encourage Visitors to Submit Contact Information — You can increase your contact and email list with social media platforms as you encourage your visitors to leave their contact info to get a better offer. Encourage visitors to leave their contact info or email address so that you can reach out to them with good offers. This call to action for visitors is an excellent strategy to increase your email list as you attract more visitors. With these contacts, you can improve your marketing. Seek to improve sales and keep customers by reaching out to them through email with great offers. Encourage your visitors to register and fill out contact forms through a link you will provide to them. You can encourage them to register with special offers or vouchers upon complete registration. Share these posts on your social media platforms to keep your customers and attract new ones.

Your Quick Start Action Step:

In this action step, we are going to outline a schedule that will keep you guided in achieving these objectives:

1. *Set up a schedule when you will be actively online to socialize with your customers. You cannot be online all 24 hours of the day, so choose the time that your particular social media platform is most active, like in the middle of the day or the evening.*

2. *Provide at least three quality posts a week and post them on your social media platforms to keep your users engaged. Plan the content weekly and spread it across the week on your websites or blogs. For example, one at the beginning of the week, one at midweek, and the last one on the weekend. You will get your customers engaged regularly with your content and keep them returning for more.*

3. *Set up promotional offers and contests at least once a month, especially at the end of the month and holidays.*

4. *Offer giveaways, price slashes, and freebies to customers on favorite holidays.*

5. *Respond to messages from customers promptly, especially inquiries and requests.*

Chapter 5:
Building Your
Brand Awareness
with Social Media
Marketing

Chapter 5: Building Your Brand Awareness with Social Media Marketing

5.1 How Social Media Marketing Can Build Your Brand

Now that you have successfully caught the attention of the right audience, you need to let them know about your product in the most enticing way. You will learn a lot in this chapter, especially regarding how you can promote your brand and increase awareness of your product.

Your brand is the total entity of your business, and it goes beyond your business name and logo. A brand includes the way you interact with your client or potential clients; anything relating to your business that gets to the end user tells a lot about your brand.

Creating awareness about your brand is a task that requires you to take your business out there to the people. With social media, the task has become more natural, and you can bring your brand to a considerable number of people with less work than in the traditional methods of marketing.

Social media can help build your brand up, and it does not matter if you are new to the industry or if the business has been running for years. You have to put your brand on social media to have any recognition nowadays; you cannot just ignore the platforms.

Companies usually have advertising departments or outsource this aspect of the business to an agency. However, this has been transformed as brands now employ social media managers to help build their brands online and manage the massive potential of customers on these platforms.

Social media marketing can help build your brand in the following ways:

- Social media will expose you to a wide range of people. Your brand will be exposed to the young and old, male and female, and people of different races and cultures.
- Your brand will be exposed to a vast number of people since there are millions (and even billions!) of people active on social media platforms. More people will become aware of your brand when you market it on social media platforms.

- Social media can expose your brand globally, which would have been an incredible feat to achieve through traditional marketing. You can reach out to anyone anywhere in the world through social media platforms, giving you global reach.
- You can make your product readily available as customers and potential clients reach out to you on social media platforms, requesting your product.
- You ensure that your brand remains relevant to social media marketing when you post and share content regularly.

5.2 The Importance of Aligning Social Media Marketing with Your Brand

You will find more companies with accounts on all of the popular social media platforms than you would have some five to ten years ago. This is because people are becoming aware of the importance of social media in building their brands.

Even companies that have been skeptical of leaving the traditional way of marketing have opted for social media marketing. This change is due to the positive impact that social media marketing has had on brand awareness and the marketing of businesses. Moreover, they have to assimilate to this new age of social media awareness so that they are not entirely out of the online world.

In this section, we are going to highlight the importance of aligning social media marketing with brand awareness. Below, we'll discuss the essence of each point:

- Social Media Is the Fastest Growing Marketing Platform — Forget television or telemarketing; social media is the fastest growing marketing platform in the world. As a marketer, you cannot ignore the statistics coming out and the success that brands have found through social media marketing strategies. As we have seen, almost everyone we know has at least one social media account. Almost everyone is on Facebook, and it has become a popular platform where friends and families meet and share pictures, thoughts, and events. Twitter has played a significant role in many events that have occurred around the world, from the

Arab Spring revolution that saw the ousting of a long-serving president in North Africa to millions of people discussing and participating in trending events like the World Cup and the Olympics, all in real-time. These are just a few examples of what these platforms have done and the global impact they have. With these events, imagine the impact social media will have on a brand if it can pull off the scale of awareness in a positive way.

- Moreover, companies have learned to use the influence these social platforms have to promote their brands on a global scale. With the right images, videos, and content, you can become influential on any of the social media platforms, and take advantage of the significant number of active users of these platforms. Moreover, think of how the number of people joining these platforms is increasing as more people register on these platforms. The potential in using these platforms with its considerable number of followers is unlimited, and you can reach your marketing peak. What age range of people do you want to reach out to? What is the location of the people you are targeting? Are you targeting men or women? Young people or older? With social media marketing, you can reach out to any of these sets of people. You can align your marketing campaigns and make an impact on your prime audience. Facebook, Twitter, and Instagram are some of the fastest growing social media networks. Twitter, Instagram, and Pinterest are popular platforms where we are seeing more young people, especially women, registering over time, while Facebook has seen an overall growth across all parameters, like age, location, culture, and business. More brands are creating Facebook and Instagram pages to showcase their companies and services. Many people choose Facebook due to its excellent features that brands can use to target audiences.

-

- <u>Take Advantage of Influencers on These Platforms</u> — Influencers are vital if you intend to build awareness about your business on social media platforms, and create successful online marketing campaigns. These influencers can promote your brand to the vast numbers of followers they have on these platforms. When you are registered on these platforms, you can connect with some of these influencers to help you market your brand and build awareness. There are different kinds of influencers you should be looking out for to help promote your business. There are famous figures such as celebrities, sports personalities, musicians, politicians, and other public figures. Then there are those with vast numbers of followers that they have managed to gain over time. The trick here is that the followers are, in a way, influenced by what these influencers post, and posting about your brand is like an endorsement. This will create more awareness about the brand as it gets accepted, which will result in an increase of leads to the business. However, in leveraging the popularity of these influencers, your brand must be credible enough for the influencers to risk their status in endorsing your brand. Also, in some cases, you have to spend money or offer some of your products or services in exchange for them to promote your products or services to their followers. So, by aligning your brand with social media marketing, you can take advantage of influencers to promote your brand and reach out to more people effectively. Identifying influencers on these popular platforms is another challenge for the successful promotion of your product. It would be best if you looked for those in the same niche as you who have enough followers and engagement on their posts. You should identify influencers in the same niche so you can promote your brand to people who will be interested in what your brand offers. You should be able to identify people that will boost your brand to your targeted audience and avoid wasting time and resources.

- Compete with Your Competitors — As social media marketing has become popular, brands and businesses have taken their efforts to the platforms. They put their names and logos on their social media platforms as they promote and create awareness of their businesses. Now, if some brands in the same niche as you have been on social media for a long time, you may have to play catch-up to meet up with them. They may have gained enough followers before you join the platforms, and you'll have to try and rival these competitors in the shortest time possible. With this in mind, aligning your social media marketing with your brand will enable your business to compete with other brands in the same niche. If you are not on social media, your brand will fall behind, and people won't find you when they search for your niche. Aligning your brand with social media marketing will enable you to compete with other brands in the same niche who are already making an impact on these platforms. Customers will gain trust and confidence in your brand when they find you online alongside other popular brands. Do not be left out in this age of social media marketing; reach out to where the audience matters on these platforms. A look at the top brands on these platforms will enable you to plan your marketing strategies. You can model your marketing campaign after that of your competitors as you learn how to manage marketing on this platform. You cannot compete with other businesses if you are not on the same playing field, so ensure that you study your competitors and learn how to reach their level.

- <u>Sell Yourself on Social Media</u> — There is a lot of gossip on social media, and you can only correct any wrong impressions made about your brand when you are on these platforms. If you are not on any of these social media platforms, you cannot manage to defend yourself against what other users say about your brand, especially if your competitors decide to play down your brand on social media. By being present on these popular platforms, you can control the narrative of your brand. You can sell your brand online in ways that suit your business and manage how you want other users to see your business. You can also converse with your customers on these platforms, and this will improve awareness of your brand. By adequately addressing your customers on these platforms when they make inquiries, you will create more knowledge about your brand. When you are on social media, you can also promote your brand effectively through your logos and the business details available to your audience. It is never a good idea to sell your brand to your target audience using another account; this will only create distrust from your audience. Aligning your brand with social media marketing creates more awareness of everything related to your brand. Your audience will become familiar with your logo, business address, and even website when you are marketing with your brand.

- <u>Meet People Interested in Your Brand</u> — If you are looking for people who will be interested in your brand, then social media marketing will help you in achieving that objective. Social media offers you the tools and ways to reach out to people who will have an interest in your brand, ultimately increasing awareness and leads. Facebook, for example, provides data that can analyze the preferences and interests of its users. You can use this available and useful data in your marketing campaigns to direct you to the audience that is most likely to be interested in your brand and business. Moreover, this will raise more awareness, as those who find your brand interesting learn about it and increase its conversion rate. With other platforms like Twitter and Instagram, the use of the proper hashtags and keywords can lead the user to your brand when they search on the platform. You can also get your brand trending on these platforms with the effective use of influencers and keywords. People who are interested in your niche and your brand will be able to find you and become aware of your brand. In this form of marketing, you should ensure that active targeted users are not only aware of your brand, but help make your brand stand out on these platforms. Make your brand stand out by making special offers and engaging your audience regularly.

- <u>Social Media Has Influencing Power Online</u> — Social media has so much power over the change in our modern-day marketing, and can control how people react to your brand. A negative review of your brand by an influencer or celebrity on any of the platforms can damage the integrity of your brand online, and it will take a lot to control and mitigate that damage. The reverse is also the case; a useful or positive review by an influencer can improve the awareness of your brand. On Twitter, for example, an impression of a brand can go viral and trend, which will make your brand visible to millions of users. This exposure would influence your product and brand either positively or negatively, depending on the reason you are trending. The remarks that people make about your brand have an influencing power over your brand. You can leverage this influencing power of social media to promote your brand by getting your event to trend. When more people are talking about your brand, it creates a buzz on social media platforms, and your event can become the trending topic for the day. When social media platforms pick up signals that you are getting more attention, your brand will be listed as trending, which will raise more curiosity.

People will want to find out about your brand or events and will join the conversation, which builds more buzz about the brand. When you align your brand with social media marketing, you can have control and manage the situation. You can encourage more people to talk about your event and share your content, creating a lot of buzz and enabling you to become a trending topic. A suitable example is asking users to share your content to become eligible for a prize or contest.

5.3 Steps on How to Build Your Brand with Social Media Marketing

You should follow the steps below to build your brand through social media marketing:

1. Set up the Right Brand Name on Social Media — The first step you have to take is to consider the brand name that you will use for your marketing on these social media platforms. It is ideal that you use your brand name on your social media platforms when registering on the platform. It becomes easier to identify with the brand name when it is similar to the name of

your business. There are few occasions when a brand name has to be different from the name on social media, such as if the name has already been taken on the social media platform. On such occasion, the brand might buy the account on the platform if the person is willing to sell the name. On the other hand, if the owner does not agree to sell the account, you may be left with no other choice but to use a different name or a variation of the brand's name. In any case, it does not encourage trust and confidence when there is a significant disparity in the name. Also, it is crucial that you carry out a thorough research on your brand name and its availability on social media platforms before you begin using the name.

2. <u>Design the Logo for Your Brand</u> — The logo is an essential aspect of your brand as it will represent your business. You will use the logo as your image in your social media account. This logo will be your brand's official image, and anywhere it is seen, it will be identified with your brand. Creating a logo should not take too much time, and you can hire the

services of a professional graphic designer to create a logo for your brand. You should provide the graphic designer with details about your brand and leave it to them to create a unique logo. You should create a logo that you are sure you are not going to change any time soon. It is essential that a logo is consistently used, so anyone who sees it will identify it with your brand. Changing the logo frequently will confuse your audience about your identity, so it is crucial to get it right the first time. Here are a few tips on building your logo:

- o Use suitable images that are relevant to your brand, products, or services.
- o Use the initials or the name of your brand if it is short enough to fit in the logo.
- o Make the logo as simple as possible.
- o Do not use too much color variation.

3. <u>Select a Suitable Social Media Platform for Your Brand</u> — Honestly, it will be difficult for you to focus on all the social media platforms in your online marketing campaign. You

cannot promote your brand successfully if you try to concentrate on all of the platforms at once. The best advice is to select, at maximum, three of these platforms, and work on them one at a time. The first step in choosing the right platform is to find out which one is most suitable for your brand. Find out which of the platforms has a higher percentage of your targeted audience in order to market your brand successfully. You cannot ignore a platform like Facebook in your branding campaign, for Facebook has excellent tools and billions of active users. Through Facebook, you have the means to create a Facebook page and group for your brand where you can quickly get your targeted audience engaged in your own space. Also, Facebook has one of the highest numbers of registered and active users online. You can find a wide range of people on Facebook, and with the data collected and analyzed, you'll be able to find your targeted audience. Thus, Facebook is one of the platforms you are advised to choose when promoting your brand online. You will also have to analyze other platforms and find the ones suitable for your brand. You could add Twitter and Instagram; they are the most popular platforms for the younger generation, and they are sufficient for trending topics and events. These platforms provide you with an entirely different way of engaging with your audience. If your brand requires images and videos in promoting to your audience, and if they are of a younger generation, then Instagram, YouTube, and Pinterest should be considered. So, in essence, you should know your audience and the best way to approach them when choosing a suitable platform.

4. <u>Create Your Account</u> — Creating an account on social media platforms is an essential aspect of creating a brand for your business. At this stage, you will have to choose how you will represent yourself online and how your audience will see you. Creating your account will determine how easy it will be for your customers to find you on these platforms. Using the right name, introducing your brand, and using the right images on your profile are

vital steps in the process. It is free to register on these social media platforms. When you register with your brand name, it will appear on the account handle. Registration also includes your business address and website name. Your contact information should include email address, office address, and website name. The use of images is also appropriate in branding your business on social media platforms. Your logo should appear on your image profile, and you can use other business images as the background of your account profile. Some platforms require that you introduce your brand in the bio segment. Here, you can write about your business and the kinds of services and products you offer. Be creative, since you want to catch the attention of your audience. It is a short introduction and does not require as much detail as you would find on a post. Your account is set and complete, and you are living on the platform and ready to promote your brand.

5. <u>Post Content and Promote Your Brand</u> — Now that you have your account all set up, the next

step is to post relevant content on the account page for your visitors. You cannot leave your social media platform without any reasonable posts to engage your visitors. Before you do anything else with the account, you have to post some relevant content about your brand. The first set of posts on your platform should be more of an introduction to your brand. It's best if you tell your visitors more about your brand using the appropriate content, images, or videos. You can post more pictures or videos of your operations and activities, or write engaging content about your operations. You can hire the services of content developers to help your brand produce the right content to engage your visitors. Create content that is relevant to your brand and posts on your social media platform, and always mention your brand in that content. Image and video content should be high quality and contain the brand logo, or at least mention the brand somewhere. You do not have to be too obvious when referring to your brand. Make it as subtle as possible while still providing the audience with quality content. Research content topics and ensure you provide your audience with facts as you enlighten and entertain them. In addition, have a regular posting schedule and stay consistent. The important thing is that you have content to engage your visitors and create awareness about your brand.

6. Encourage People to Follow and Like Your Account — You have completed your account creation and posted some relevant content on the pages or timeline. The next step is to get people to follow or like your social media account, depending on the platform you chose. Getting people to follow you is one of the most challenging tasks in building your brand through social media marketing; you have to prove to the audience that they stand to gain more when they follow your account. Moreover, this is why you need some exciting content on your account before you proceed to promote the brand on social media. With some relevant posts and content, you can start inviting people to follow or like your social media account. You should start with friends

and family by importing them from your contacts to like and follow your account. Inviting your family and friends is easy to do on social media; you are provided with the option to import contacts from your Facebook account, Twitter account, Instagram account, or other social media accounts, including importing from your contacts, to invite them to follow your new account. Use this tool to import as many contacts as possible to gain some instant followers. At this stage, you should encourage your friends and family to invite people from their contacts to follow your new accounts as well. Reaching out to people you are familiar with is the first step towards gaining followers as you build your brand using social media marketing. With this process, you may have gotten a handful of followers, and expect more as you encourage them to share content with friends and share on the page. If you have enough exciting content, people begin to share your material, and your scope expands beyond your friend and family. That is the first step of promoting your brand using social media platforms. The next step is to carry out the extended promotion of your brand by targeting audiences who will likely be interested in your brand by using data analysis from Facebook. You can also use the paid ads on Facebook to target audiences with high positive results of brand marketing. Twitter and Instagram also have similar paid ads to increase the awareness of your brand to targeted audiences. Take advantage of these tools and reach out to as many people as possible.

7. <u>Join Groups and Discussion Boards</u> — A great way to promote your brand is to be active among people of similar niches or interests. You can create your brand's group on a platform like Facebook and get people of similar interests to partake and join in. You will have these people discussing related issues while promoting your brand. As you join other groups of similar interests, and expand your horizons and contacts, join their discussion boards to promote your brand. You can find so many groups with similar interests on

Facebook and other platforms, and you can join as many as you want to reach out to people. Participating in group discussion exposes your brand to more people. Engage with them in factual debate and, at times, get personal with your audience to create friendly conversations. On platforms like Twitter and Instagram, you can use hashtags to join the general discussion and give your brand more exposure.

8. Build a Beneficial Partnership with Influencers — On every social media platform, there are those who can influence matters, events, and discussions both positively or negatively. These people are called influencers, and they have a huge follower base that trusts their input. These influencers can determine what people will think about your brand and can ensure you get positive recognition online. You should look for these influencers and bloggers and build beneficial partnerships with them to promote your brand. Understand that you can also create a favorable relationship with other brands where you share links on your blogs or

social media platforms and get the same treatment in return. The important thing is that your brand should provide quality products and services. With quality products and services, you do not have to sort through people online to push your products for your brand. However, you might need to spend money on convincing some influencers to help you promote your brand on social media platforms.

9. Study Other Brands Carrying out Social Media Marketing — The next step in building your brand using social media marketing is studying your competitors and their strategies. You do not necessarily need to copy their policies, but learn what works and does not work so you can get it right with your marketing. In studying your competitors, you can plan your strategies and understand how to promote your brand with your competitors in mind. If your competitors are offering a 5% slash in prices, you can increase yours to a 10% discount to win over more customers. Knowing what your competitors are up to will keep you prepared

on how to act and promote your brand. You can also check out how others have managed to build their brands using social media marketing. These brands do not necessarily need to be in your niche, but you can still learn how they carry out their marketing strategies. You can always learn from the best strategies to help your brand.

10. Be Positive and Consistent — Everyone loves to follow people who make them feel happy on social media, and this is the aim of most brands. They seek to make their audiences happy with their posts, especially when they offer solutions to problems. Your brain aims to make your audience happy, and you should portray this on your platform. Always stay positive in your posts and discussions with your audience. Even if they seem angry, a positive disposition will not only calm the customer but also portrays your brand in a positive light to others on the platform. Ensure you post the solution and article that will engage your audience and keep them informed. It helps if you are consistent in your activities

on social media marketing. Inconsistencies will lead to distrust, so always check for facts before you post content. You do not want to post content and have to retrieve or retract it in just a few days. Inconsistencies will make people move on to other brands for more accurate solutions and information. Branding and marketing are essential aspects that will boost your business effectively. Getting in-depth knowledge of branding and marketing will help you align your business through the use of social media marketing.

Your Quick Start Action Step:

Listed below are some quick start action steps that you should take to kickstart your brand marketing through social media marketing. To learn more about effective branding and how it can help your business, check out "Branding and Marketing," which you can own when you visit the online store.

1. *Register with your brand name and logo on the appropriate number of social media platforms that you can handle.*

2. *Post relevant content or get someone to manage your content on your platform.*

3. *Set up a simple marketing strategy with a daily routine and stick to it.*

4. *Be consistent with your posts on your popular social media platforms.*

Leave a Review:

As an independent author with a small marketing budget, reviews are my livelihood on this platform. If you enjoyed this book, I'd appreciate it if you leave your honest feedback. I love hearing from my readers, and I personally read every single review. You can do so by visiting the book page on Amazon.com.

Chapter 6:
Social Media
Content That
Engages

Chapter 6: Social Media Content That Engages

6.1 How Great Social Media Content Can Improve Engagement

Content that engages will not only draw the attention of online users; they will also be interested in reading through the text, regardless of length.

To achieve the purpose of better user engagement, your content must contain relevant information that is not just about your brand or products; it must be of value to the reader. This means posting engaging and well-researched content that has beneficial information to your target audience.

There is a feature on most social media platforms that enables you to share content with your friends. One quality of engaging social media content is that it gets a lot of reposts.

It is essential that you carry out a thorough research on topics that are related to your brand and compose informative articles on these topics. You should ensure that this content is original and engaging to promote your brand and keep your audience on your platform.

Content does encourage responsiveness on your platform and boosts awareness of your brand. Some companies hire professional writers and content developers to create engaging material for their brands to attract and keep customers.

Social media content can improve engagement and responsiveness in the following ways:

- Attracts an audience with articles or content that provide a solution, so they rely on your brand to offer them solutions.
- Encourages discussion on your social media platforms as your audience share their views and opinions related to the content.
- Encourages followers sharing your content with other people, especially when they find the content enlightening and helpful.
- Encourages people to follow your brand for updates of quality content, thus improving engagement.
- It helps your brand build authority in its niche

as people are encouraged to approach your brand on relevant issues.

- It helps drive traffic to your platform and increases engagement.

After setting up your social media account, you have to set up a schedule for posting content to encourage engagement. You should be smart about posting content, so you don't bore your audience, and that is why you should be creative and innovative with it.

You should post content about different aspects of your niche to ensure that your posts do not become too monotonous or similar. A good way around this is to arrange the content in three to four categories and post them at regular intervals. For example, you could have inspirational content, how-to content, promotional content, and informative content. Arrange it in such a way that it is easy to post them in turns and at regular intervals to keep your content interesting, engaging, and fresh.

6.2 The Importance of Planning Social Media Content to Branding

Delivering quality content is an essential aspect of

social media marketing, and that is why companies are employing content developers to handle their marketing campaigns online. Developing content is not as easy as many people may think. However, factual content will help build trust and confidence in your brand.

There is a lot of work involved in developing content and posting this content on social media platforms. You do not want to waste time and resources on producing content that may have only a little impact based on the responsiveness on the post.

You have to spend time researching suitable topics that your audience will find interesting and then examining the topic thoroughly to ensure that you provide facts that your audience can digest. Content that contains false information will only damage your brand name and cause you to lose credibility. Being content aware is why you have to be careful with what you post online.

Below are some of the reasons why planning your social media content is essential to branding your business:

- <u>Good Content Attracts a Larger Audience</u> —

One of the benefits of quality social media content is that it attracts a larger audience and creates more awareness of your brand. Your customers will share any quality content they come across on your platforms on their social media platforms. When other people view this exciting content, they will want to know more about your brand, which will also increase your audience. When you are preparing and planning content to post on social media, ensure that the content is of high quality because it will be bearing your brand. No more posting content to feed your visitors. Ensure that the content is impactful and will push them to share with other people. When visitors see quality content from your brand, they will likely want to check out the other content on your platform. Having great content will increase visitors who are eager to digest more quality articles offered by your brand. Don't post any half-baked articles on your social media account; take the time to research and produce quality content for your audience.

- <u>Visitors Will Spend More Time on Your</u>

Platform — Brands love their visitors to spend more time on their platforms, and that is another parameter to determine if your brand is engaging your visitors enough. If visitors find exciting content on your platform, they will spend more time on your platform, which is a massive boost to your social media marketing campaign. Visitors will spend more time on your platform if they take the time to read the content and then check out other posts. In the process, these visitors become familiar and comfortable with your brand and begin to trust your brand. There is a chance that these visitors will be converted to sales when they spend more time on your platform. When checking out your analytics tool, you can see which posts have more visitors, and you can use this data to determine what your audience likes and how to use it to boost your brand. Therefore, in preparing content for your social media branding campaign, keep in mind that you want to engage visitors longer on the platform. Make sure your articles contain enough material to keep them reading for a while, but not so long that they'll get bored.

- Increases Expectation from Your Brand — With quality content, your visitors will now trust you to deliver quality products and services, and this is one of the most critical aspects of social media content marketing. It tells your visitors what to expect from your brand, and with rich content, there will be more patronage of your brand. It is equally likely that you will provide quality content, as well as quality products and services. Quality becomes the keyword for your brand, and this expectation will lead to more visitors as your brand becomes known for its high quality. However, you have to uphold the standard you have set for your brand with high-quality content in order to keep your customers. Quality content will build trust; the customers will be assured that you know the business well enough to put up quality content. This trust and confidence will then be linked to your services and products, together with the impression of your ability to produce consistently. Carry out proper research and only provide accurate facts in your articles and posts. Make sure that pictures and videos are of high quality as you build trust with your visitors.

- <u>Your Brand Becomes an Authority in the Niche</u> — When you post quality content, this will make you an authority in the industry or niche, and the client will believe in what you have to say. You become an influencer as your content influences a considerable number of people in the industry, and you can achieve this by providing quality content. Through the process of delivering quality content, you will have to carry out research on various topics related to your industry. During this process, you will also be building your knowledge on a wide range of topics in the industry. Your experience will become vast as you share smart, quality content with your followers. People like to share interesting and informative content, and when they do, the people they are sharing the content with become aware of the source of the content. They take note of your brand as a source of authentic and intelligent content and regard you as an authority in the industry. This saved mental picture is one way that brands become an authority in the industry; showcasing quality products and services as well as the in-depth knowledge of the industry it's in. People get to appreciate this knowledge and depend on the brand to learn more about the industry. With the knowledge you acquire, you can help your visitors with their inquiries and answer questions posted on your platform.

- Social Media Content Increases Engagement — All brands want customers and visitors to engage with and respond to them on their platforms. One way to achieve this is to provide them with quality content. There will be a lot of traffic on your platform as visitors digest the quality content and share it on their social media accounts. Quality content usually has more engagement; you will have more comments as visitors share their opinions and ask questions after reading the article. This engagement builds up more responses as you communicate with these visitors and open up a discussion board on the topics where they share opinions. It is crucial that you participate in the conversations created by any of your posts, especially in the comment sections. Keep the comments going for as long as you can and encourage further engagement as you answer questions raised by your visitors.

6.3 Steps for Creating Engaging Content on Social Media

In this section of this book, we are going to guide you on the steps you should take to create engaging content. Quality content is more than just writing and posting articles, and posting images and videos on your social media platforms.

To engage your visitors and readers and build your brand, you need to follow these steps:

1. Plan Your Content — It takes planning and time to dish out quality content regularly. First, you have to draw up a suitable plan of when to post, what to post, and how to post the content. A plan enables you to stay consistent in your content marketing with social media. With a plan, you will become regular in your posting as you set the number of posts per week and the times to post during the week. Planning

involves searching for the right topics to post and researching keywords and links to use for your content. The plan may also include designating certain subjects to writers if you have content writers working for you. Planning is the first step in finding success with your social media content marketing.

2. <u>Research Your Target Audience</u> — The next step is to understand what your audience will be interested in, and how it will help you grow your brand. You do not want to waste time and resources on creating content which your audience will not find interesting. While researching suitable, relevant content, you can check up on your competitors and make a note of the articles that have the highest response. You can check out the structures of these posts and use them as a guideline when you post on your social media platforms. Researching also involves studying the articles you intend to post. You research the topic, search for the right keywords to use, and decide what will make up the content of the post. The content of the post may include words, images, and videos

as you look for something engaging. This step is crucial in creating an engaging post. The primary research you should do at this stage includes:

- o Topics that your targeted audience will find interesting to increase responses on your post.
- o The content will make up those topics, including images and videos.
- o You are picking the best time to post the content on social media platforms to ensure maximum engagement.

3. Create the Content — There is even more to creating engaging content after you have found the right topics and keywords to use. Creating content requires that writers have an understanding of the topics and how to use keywords for search engine optimization. Most brands do pay writers to help them create quality content even after they have researched the right topics and keywords. These writers are professionals, and they know how to input the keywords accurately in the content to

ensure the proper keyword density and accurate readability score. All these efforts are geared towards increasing the organic search of the article. In your article, embed social media tools that will enable your post to be shared easily online through the social media shortcuts that you provide in the article. Thus, if you keep search engine optimization in mind when you create your content, your post can be shared easily on these platforms. When these audiences search for your post online and find it interesting and engaging, they will share it on their social media platforms using the available social media buttons in the article.

4. Moreover, we can see why we need to put a lot of consideration and preparation for creating our article. Understanding how people can engage our articles through search engine optimization can also increase engagement in social media branding and marketing. If you cannot afford to hire the services of a professional writer, you can learn how to write a comprehensive article to boost awareness online. There are books and articles you can

find online that will help you improve your writing enough to create quality content.

5.

6. <u>Images and Videos for Your Content</u> — Content with pictures and videos have more engagement than content with no images or videos. Images have a way of attracting an audience, especially on platforms like Facebook or Twitter. It is a fact that tweets with pictures and videos have more clicks than tweets without them. Use high-quality images, which you can find on popular websites for free images. You can find images on these websites related to your brand and use them in your content to increase audience interest. Make use of a smartphone with a high-quality camera to take images of your products or services being offered and post them to engage your audience. Videos are also essential tools to increase audience response through content on social media. You can post videos of your brand or customers making use of your products. You can also post videos on how to use your

products or how people can get your services. Ensure that the videos are top quality and not too long. Otherwise, your audience may get bored. It is easy to make high-quality videos by utilizing a smartphone equipped with a high-quality camera.

7. Post Reviews and Feedback from Customers — Your content can be more engaging when you post reviews from customers about your products or services. This will, in turn, encourage other customers to share their experiences with your brand and increases engagement with your content. People also like to check out these reviews to learn more about your brand, and if you have what it takes for them to buy from you. It is an excellent way of increasing engagement and promoting your brand through customer participation, especially when you have something great to offer. You can get more activity when you post feedback for customers online. You can relate to these customers in the content posted, engaging them while other visitors observe and learn more about your brand.

8. Post Contests and Gifts Online — Customers love gifts, and you can attract them with content that offers rewards or competitions to win prizes. Post content that offers gifts, especially on holidays to boost engagement. Brands often use these promotional strategies to increase awareness and responsiveness on the platform. Promote content that offers price slashes and giveaways, and observe how quickly the interest in your products and services grows. Competitions are also suitable ways to increase engagement, as visitors will have fun playing games to win prizes. You can engage a larger audience through competition, such as asking some simple questions online and offering brand products or services to those that got the right answers.

9. Encourage Customers to Take Surveys — Asking your customers to take surveys online and answer simple questions about your brands is another way of engaging them online. Make this as simple and exciting as possible; you want your customers and potential customers to have fun taking these surveys.

Surveys should be as short as possible to avoid visitors quitting the survey halfway through. It also helps to make the questions interesting for your audience; get to know more about them through these surveys.

10. Post Articles at the Right Time — When posting content on social media, you need to study the most active period of your social media platform. There are certain times of the day when social media platforms are very busy, depending on the location of people you are targeting and the age group of those people. It is a well-known fact that more people are more active on social media during the day rather than at night. It makes sense to post during the day to ensure maximum exposure for your post. In this case, you have to be aware of where your target audience is geographically located, and ensure that your post reaches them at the proper time. With Facebook ads, your post will appear on the timelines of your targeted audience when they are online. If you want to post directly to your timeline, then do it at the time of the day when more people are

actively online to get the most exposure.

11. <u>Post Funny Content</u> — Another proven way that you can create engagement on social media is by introducing content that will amuse your target audience. We are not asking you to magically become a comedian or post content that will have your reader rolling on the floor with laughter. Just introduce a little bit of amusement or humor in your online write-ups. Apart from successfully catching the attention of your audience, they will be willing to read everything you have in your articles, and your followers will always look forward to your posts. It helps if you keep them satisfied by posting new content regularly.

12. <u>Accept Guest Posts</u> — You will get more responses from guest posters when you open your platform for other people to post content. You will need to vet the guest poster to ensure that they are top quality by checking on their blogs or previous posts. It is also recommended that you accept posts from guests with large numbers of followers, or guest posters who are

influential. A guest poster with a huge influence can help increase engagement on your brand as they share the content with their huge audiences. This will, in turn, raise awareness about your brand as you become exposed to their followers.

13. <u>Employ Social Media Managers</u> — Some professionals are available to help promote and increase engagement on social media through content development. These professionals use their expertise, along with the tools available on these platforms, to help improve your brand and increase engagement. They know how to create appealing content on social media, and they can help you manage your social media platforms. Top brands have social media managers dedicated solely to them, which goes a long way in showing the importance of these managers in promoting your brand with engaging content.

Your Quick Start Action Step:

To learn more about effective content and content marketing, and how it can help your business, check out "Content Marketing," which you can own when you visit the online store. Here are some quick steps you can take to create engaging content for your brand:

1. *Look for an informative and relevant topic that you know will catch the attention of social media users. Choose a catchy and SEO-optimized title. For instance, if you sell mattresses, you could use a phrase like "sleeping positions that cure insomnia".*

2. *Start your content with something captivating that will keep your reader engrossed. You can tell them a story of how a man's chronic back pain disappeared in two weeks after he slept on a particular mattress!*

3. *Add a little bit of amusement and humor to your writing.*

4. *Look for high-quality images or videos that are related to your topic and include them in your posts.*

5. *Add offers or special gifts to your post to attract more potential customers.*

6. *Mention reviews and feedback about the post to get more attention to your article.*

7. *Share and reshare the content on all of the social media platforms where you are promoting your brand.*

Chapter 7:
Using Facebook

Chapter 7: Using Facebook

7.1 Definition of Facebook

It's unlikely that you haven't heard of Facebook, and you probably even have an account. However, how would you reply, if anyone, possibly someone very close to you, asks for a precise, meaningful, and direct definition of Facebook? Would you say: "It is a social networking site?"

Facebook is indeed a social networking site, but in the marketing world, a more precise definition is highly essential. Why? It gives more than an overview; it provides an expansive view of some key elements of Facebook itself. Thus, from the description, a reader or a potential user of the social tool can be aware of varying degrees of opportunities from which they can benefit.

Put simply, Facebook is a globally-recognized social networking website that offers registered users the ability to create profiles, send messages, and upload videos and photos to aid communication between their family and friends, colleagues, and others.

Undeniably, Facebook offers anyone with the desire to utilize it the opportunity to promote and smooth interactions between two or more people, as long as they have the means and opportunity to create an account. With Facebook, you can stay connected and share and express things of paramount importance to anyone.

When Mark Zuckerberg and some other Harvard University classmates founded Facebook in 2004, their sole aim was to make the world more open and connected; you can see the gold mine for marketers!

Facebook comes with several beneficial public features. All these features are sources of aid to businesses and offer relevant promotions to companies. These features include Marketplace, groups, events, pages, and presence technology. We'll briefly highlight some of these elements to give you an overview of how each feature works and how they have an overreaching effect on business:

- *Marketplace:* This feature offers members or users the ability to create posts, read posts, and respond to any classified ads to buy or sell items.
- *Groups:* This feature helps app users with common interests locate, find, and interact with each other.

- *Pages:* This excellent feature allows members to create and promote pages that are designated to a specific topic.
- *Events:* This feature enables members to publicize an event, invite guests, and track anyone who plans to attend.
- *Presence Technology:* Members can use this feature to investigate who on their contact list is online, and start a chat with them.

Additionally, the Facebook wall is also an active bulletin board. A business person using this application can leave text, a photo, or a video as a message. However, it should be noted that there are several privacy options that members of Facebook can utilize, so with diligence and reasonableness, safety and security can be guaranteed.

There are certain social media content pieces that a business person should create and post on Facebook. How do you identify the important content? And how can you determine which content will be engaging? Read further and see how the next section explains eleven distinct types of social media content.

7.2 What Kind of Content to Post on Facebook

Many marketers today deal with creative block. Right before them, they have a deadline to meet, and coming up with a single post—a post that will be regarded as an individual campaign post, becomes a severe problem with which they have to wrestle.

Can you relate to those people mentioned above? If yes, then don't panic! Listed below are some inspirational compilations. With these, even when facing zero motivation, you can come up with engaging and surprising content. Does that bring relief? Then, I'll repeat it: you are where you should be.

The list that you will go through will help you find something unique that neither current nor prospective customers have seen before, regardless of where they are most active.

However, before launching ahead, using the right tools is just as important as the steps you will soon learn about. Examples of such tools are:

- Social Media Calendar Template
- Social Media Strategy Checklist
- Mapping Out Posting Schedule

These tools allow you to make plans on your posts beforehand, design an intensive strategy for all of your social media content, and learn how to map out a posting plan, respectively.

With this knowledge, you can better understand the types of content to post on Facebook. Let's find out!

- *Business Blog Posts* — If your company runs a blog, this is for you! However, how do you make them work? Link your blog to your business Facebook account. You will end up bringing your blog to a public stage where it will get many views. Plus, it's from your business, so no one is going to question the content, and then you can give top quality services. Note: Be sure that any articles are excellently written, valuable, and engaging to your audience. One idea is ensuring that you give posts that are known to be actionable, such as "How to" articles.

- *Question Posts* — Don't post blog posts all the time. Have time for questions. Questions? Yes! One way to keep your audience engaged is to roll out thrilling, meaningful, and well-thought-out questions. The questions you ask should be thought-provoking and lead to more questions. For example, you can know your viewers' opinions on the type of content posted on your page. For instance, you could ask: "what material would you want to see featured here next?" From the comments, pick the most popular response.

- *Customer Reviews and Testimonials* — If your business has lots of fans, then you can professionally flaunt their positive feedback and still make your post count on Facebook. By posting reviews and testimonials, you are indirectly letting their voices be heard, and their thoughts and strong opinions would be shared on social media. All you need to accomplish this is to display phrases or go more professional by developing a graphic that has their testimonial on it. Nevertheless, when presenting this, always be sure to add their name. Doing this will let the readers confirm the validity of the testimony.

- *Answers to Frequently Asked Questions* — Now, this type of content requires that you are observant, but the beauty of this is indeed immeasurable! Each time you are either on your blog or your Facebook page, create time to investigate the questions you receive. Then, determine whether that particular question is asked often. Rather than spend the whole day answering each person, cleverly convert that question into the title of a post. This way, you are sharing the answer through a post on Facebook. Pin the answer to the top of your social media page for easy recognition and identification.

- *Live Videos* — Making use of videos on Facebook is also appealing to those business people marketing through social media. However, it isn't just about uploading edited videos; you can also go live on Facebook. Stick to this live video pattern. For instance, if you have the resources, do it once a week. Moreover, be specific about the day of the week you will be doing it. It could be tagged 'Monday Motivational Tips', or on a Friday, 'Weekend

Facts'. Creativity is necessary to ensure that you tailor these to your business.

- *Inspirational or Motivational Quotes* — Inspirational quotes can be cheesy at times but used correctly, you can benefit from their flexibility. You can accomplish this by utilizing quotes from industry leaders that your audience wouldn't frown upon, but this will require some underground work. Make it a point only to use quotes that will resonate with your audience.

- *Groundbreaking Company Accomplishment* — This is another way to post on Facebook. Your audience, most notably your fan base, wants to see you attain success. Do not hesitate to share this success with them. Besides, showing your success reinforces conviction in potential customers, since they have the assurance that you are progressing. Think about the awards you've won, the peak of loyal customers that you have gained, an update in the company's mode of operation, or anything else you've accomplished.

- *Request Customer Feedback* — Your posts on Facebook can and should always include customer feedback requests. There may be times when you are unsure about how your audience will react to an entirely new feature, business event, or upgrade. Your post can validate either your audience is in the agreement or rejects the change. Here are some examples of feedback requests:

    o *"We want to design a custom label feature; would you like it?" (Alternatively, you could say: "Tell us what you think!")*

    o *"In what ways do you think our customer service could be improved?"*

    o *"We are holding an event next week; are you interested in coming?"*

    The point is, there are many questions you can ask and get feedback on. Treading this path is an incredible way to reach out and build a loyal fan base.

- *Post Your Company's Culture* — You want viewers and users to have a straight and unadulterated view of your business. Sharing your authenticity is a better way to showcase your business by ensuring that you feature a culture post. A culture post is an image or article that reveals what your business stands for, or what it is all about. You can tactfully show your company's swiftness to work or the unique abilities of your employees. For instance, show a behind-the-scenes photo of your employees at work in their safety gear. Alternatively, write an article on how your company handles a specific request. This post on Facebook will go a long way in establishing trust and confidence in your business. Thus, you'll acquire more customers, either with a single post or several posts.

- *Curated Content* — If you choose to use this post on your Facebook business account, please don't avoid giving credit where credit is due. Don't use this pattern all the time, but it's not a bad idea to use it once in a while. Moreover, ensure that you use it because you found that it is precisely what you need and cost-effective. Therefore, all you need is to share the written content relevant to your niche and give credit to the original poster. Don't just post without giving proper credit; you don't want to damage your reputation, do you?

- *Memes or GIFs* — Your Facebook post doesn't have to be perceived as too rigid or void of fun. Your audience wants laughter, too. In addition to the images you've been sharing with your audience on Facebook, you can also use memes and GIFs. When you do, you are piling fun in those skeletal posts and filling them with meat. People can't resist memes and GIFs, so they pause, learn, and laugh before scrolling further. Just keep in mind that GIFs showcase your company's personality, and keep you relevant and fun. Don't be afraid to use GIFs; they are commonly used by companies today.

With the eleven steps analyzed above, you shouldn't have any problems creating sizzling content or posts on Facebook. However, did you know that using Facebook ads can help you generate more potential consumers and even help you retain your fan base? Next, we will look at the simple steps involved in creating ads on Facebook.

7.3 How to Create Ads on Facebook

You'd be wrong in thinking that all the free social media posts are sufficient in getting your posts seen on Facebook; they are not enough.

Let's take a look at this picture, and you'll get the idea. Let's say your business is "Tune A," and you want to target a town, "New Town." Now, you researched the population of "New Town" and discovered that the population is 30,000.

Out of that figure of 30,000, how many people do you want to hear about your product? Be honest with yourself, would you be happy with only 5,000 people from that city? Most likely not! You'd want to scale up to 15,000, if not more.

Now, what's the point? Some Facebook users will see your free posts and content, but if you desire a wider reach, then paying for Facebook ads is inevitable. Currently, many media strategists are quickly learning how to leverage Facebook ads. If you don't know yet, now is the time to give it a try.

It's no exaggeration that Facebook ads have become

one of the most instant means of influencing the reach of your content. Thus, every business person who wants to make the best use of social media, specifically Facebook, must learn this aspect.

You probably have questions. The leading, of course, is: how can I get it done? You may also want to know whether the steps involved are straightforward enough for implementation. Furthermore, if you want to know if the increase in engagement is worth the cost, you can rest assured that you'll get the value of your hard-earned money.

Now, we're set to share with you everything you need to know about Facebook ads, and we'll unravel the knots that make it hard to understand. Let's start right now!

Step 1: *Set Goals for Your Facebook Ads* — You need to get each step right. Hence, each step counts. Before you begin to launch or create any advertisements, it is imperative that you determine what you need, what you intend to achieve, and why you are advertising. If you are ready, quickly ask these three wh- questions now. Moreover, provide your answer. In doing this, you have a target; your goals will help you conveniently and expertly track your progress. But is this path reasonable? Let's take this example. Let's assume you want to see an increase in the downloads of your business's mobile application via Facebook ads. Set a goal for the first month, and you will reach a peak of 100 downloads. Apart from easily tracking your progress, what you've done will relieve you of so much stress. If you aren't sure of some goals, highlighted below are five of the leading ones:

- Increase traffic to your company's website through Facebook
- Assist in generating new leads
- Increase the reach of the company's content on Facebook
- Increase the attendance at events
- Sky-high engagement/responsiveness on your Facebook page

Setting goals will give you an appealing start! Make them simple and easy to apply.

Step 2: *Move to Facebook Ads Manager* — If you are entirely new to Facebook ads, then this might be strange to you. Let's break it down. Think about any Facebook ad campaign you have ever seen or heard of;

they all run through the Facebook Ads Manager - a tool that can be accessed through a direct link on Facebook.com/ads. Alternatively, on the drop-down menu of your Facebook accounts, you can click "Manage Ads." The last option is for you to click on any of the CTAs that you find on your Facebook page. You can decide to use the three patterns interchangeably, or pick the one that's most straightforward for you. Then, what's next? In the Ads Manager, start your navigation. You will first begin with the menu on the left-hand side of the page. With your first ad, you should notice one green button in the top-right corner of the page; click on it. Now, you've started the journey of Facebook ads. I'm sure you know that this isn't the stopping point. This step is where the goals you've identified earlier become applicable.

Step 3: *Select Your Objectives* — When you click on the green button, you've set the stage. When you click on "Create a Facebook Ad," you head straight to a page where you select the objective for your campaign. There are several options in this section that you might want to achieve. In this stage, you need to set up your marketing objective. There are several ways of tackling an ad campaign on Facebook. They can be classified into three sections:

1. *Awareness* — In this section, highlight the objectives that will stimulate interest in your business product or services. The options include:

   - *Boost your posts*
   - *Reach people near you*
   - *Increase your reach*
   - *Increase brand awareness*
   - *Promote your page*

This awareness ad type is essential for anyone with a small budget, and you can have a return of 4,000 people per $1 per day.

2. *Consideration* — This type of objective is appropriate if you desire prospects or customers that instantly start thinking about your business as soon as they see it, and if you want them to unearth more information. Under these ads, there are:

   - *Send people to a destination on or off Facebook*
   - *Collect leads for your business*

- *Get to install your app*
- *Get video view*
- *Raise attendance at your event*

3. *Conversion* — This third type of objective motivates people who are interested in your business to make a purchase or start using your products and services. This type has five sections, including:

   - *Increase conversions on your website*
   - *Get people to visit your shops*
   - *Increase engagement in your app*
   - *Promote a product or catalog*
   - *Get people to claim your offer*

With the right goal in mind, you will surely select the best objective. When you choose the right marketing objective, you are required to give your campaign a name. Add the name, then click continue.

Step 4: *Define Your Audience and Budget* — There are two significant aspects to this. One is customizing your target audience, and the second is setting your budget. Let's begin with the first one:

Phase 1: Customizing Your Target Audience — Several demographics will be customized. They are based on these categories:

- *Location - input your country, state, city, zip code, and address*
- *Age*
- *Language*
- *Gender*
- *Interests - include your target's interests, pages they like, activities, and other closely linked topics.*
- *Connections - select the ad to all people; you can even narrow it down to those connected to Buffer, or those not linked to Buffer*
- *Behaviors - device usage, purchase attitude, and intent of purchase*

Additionally, you can choose to select advanced targeting options. This option allows you to include or exclude some users who are connected with your business events, pages, or apps. Furthermore, you can choose custom audiences to re-target those who have already visited your business. You should find this straightforward, but if you don't, here is a practical example for proper understanding:

> *Task: Choose an Audience for a Buffer Ad*
>
> *Location: United States*
>
> *Language(s): English (US)*
>
> *Age: 18-70*
>
> *Excluded: Users Who Already Liked Buffer*
>
> *Interests: Social Media*

Phase 2: Setting Your Budget — The next action to take after selecting your target audience is to declare your budget. You have to choose the amount you want to spend on your ad. There are a few things you have to remember; setting a budget caters for the overall money you'd want to spend. There are two basic ways of setting the budget:

- *Daily - indicates the average amount spent daily*
- *Lifetime - indicates the maximum fee that will be spent overall during the*

period or lifetime of your advert set

Crosscheck all you've inputted and make sure of your budget and targets. If everything has been confirmed, move to the next step.

Step 5: *Create Your Advertisement* — At this stage, you get to select the image/video, headline, body text, and precise area where your ad will be displayed on Facebook. Facebook limits the text to 90 characters, so you have to be crafty to write short, quality words. These short texts appear above your images or videos. There are two basic ways to create the advertisement:

1. *Use an Existing Post* — If your principal aim is to boost your existing posts that have been previously used, this is the way to go. First, select the "Use Existing Post" option from the Facebook Ads Manager dashboard. From there, you will choose an individual post from your desired page to serve as your ad.
2. *Create a New Ad* — To start, select the format you want to use for your ad. There are currently five different formats for ads:
   - *Carousel: Creates an advertisement with two or more scrollable videos or*

images

- *Single Video: Creates an ad with one video*
- *Canvas: Involves storytelling in a more immersive style by merging images and videos*
- *Slideshow: Creates a looping video ad with up to 10 images*
- *Single Image: Can create up to 6 variants of your ads using a single image*

It should be noted that the formats you select are based on the objective you chose during step 3.

When you are done selecting your format, you need to include the content—videos, images, and content—to your ad. Just ensure that you make your images and copy enticing enough, so people don't hesitate to click. Ideally, you will find the specifications for the image or video placed next to the area on the screen where you upload your content.

Step 6: *Choose Your Ad Placement* — We are a step closer to the final part. Here, ad placement defines where your ad is displayed. With Facebook Ads, you can choose in which locations you want your ad to be displayed. Typically, Facebook ads appear on Facebook's mobile News Feed, right column, and desktop News Feed. At least for the first time, implement Facebook's recommended default placement for the objective you've chosen earlier to help you get the best possible results at a cost-effective rate. Although, that doesn't mean that you can't select your placements. Click the link below for more guidance on how to get that done:

https://www.facebook.com/pages/creation/

Step 7: *Place Your Order* — At this stage, your ad is ready to launch. All you need to do is submit your ad by clicking on the "Place order" button. You will find this button at the right-hand corner of the page. Upon submission, the ad will be reviewed by Facebook. If it meets the requirements, it can then go live. Facebook will even send you a confirmation email as soon as it is live.

Your Quick Start Action Step:

With the practical steps analyzed above, when, exactly, is the right time for implementation?

Choosing the best time may concern you, but don't worry! Here are some quick start action steps that you should blend into the system to get what you want and avoid getting stuck as a reader.

1. *Get a notebook and a pen handy, then write down your goals. The process can take about 2-3 hours. It all depends on the goals of your ad and how many there are.*

2. *The next day, spend at least 2 hours confirming whether your goals are in line. Thus, there will be no alterations.*

3. *Having identified your goals, use the next day to think about your budget. Write down how much you can afford and how long the ad fee can go. If your budget isn't sufficient, think about how you can up the scale and work it out.*

4. *Get all of your tools and files, images, and videos ready the following week. You should spend a week on this in order to come up with quality content.*

5. *The following week, as soon as your tools and files are ready for launch, set up the ads, and go live!*

6. *Track your progress and repeat the process when your first ads turn out a success.*

Chapter 8:
Using Instagram

Chapter 8: Using Instagram

8.1 Definition of Instagram

You'd probably don't need an expert to tell you what Instagram is. You've likely heard of it several times. Just like Facebook, it is a universal social networking app. Even though it is a tool for individuals, some understand that businesses can use it as well.

Instagram is defined as a free social network platform, and it is an online photo-sharing application. This application allows users to edit and upload photos and short videos via a mobile app. Furthermore, users add captions to each of their posts and use hashtags and location-based geotags to index these posts, ensuring searchability by other users within the app.

When a user posts, they appear on their followers' Instagram feeds, and they can also be seen by the public when tagged by geotags or hashtags. Similar to other social media networks, Instagram offers users the ability to like, comment, send private messages to their Instagram Direct Feature, and bookmark posts.

Interestingly, Instagram was acquired by Facebook in 2012, and that establishes the trust that social media experts and business owners can use Instagram for advertising! This photo-sharing app allows companies to open business accounts to promote their brands and products. They can also have both democratic engagement and impression metrics.

Statistics, at present, reveal that there are more than 1 million advertisers globally who employ the use of Instagram to share stories and powerfully drive unprecedented business results. In a new development, 60% of users of Instagram admit that they locate new products via the app.

With all of these facts, it's clear that the app is made for business promotion; you certainly wouldn't argue that fact. Would you? You'll be even convinced of its potential boost to businesses when you consider some of the features explained below.

You don't have to be a professional to master these features, and the detailed, step-by-step guide in the final section of this chapter is easily understood. However, before that, let's explore the complete list of features:

- *Video Features* — These are regular video posts, but they are limited to 60 seconds. Additionally, you can add filters, include captions, and tag your location before sharing the post.

- *Stories Feature* — This is a bit similar to Snapchat. It allows users to add clips of video to a story that users can view for 24 hours before they disappear.
- *Push Notifications* — This hidden feature allows followers to add notifications from your business. If users enable notifications for your account, then when you post updates related to new product launches, promotions, or deals, you can earn additional sales.
- *Favorite Filters* — There are about 40 filters available on Instagram to enable creativity when posting either videos or photos. However, ensure that you maintain consistency.
- *Geo-tagged Content* — If your business is a brick-and-mortar business, then this is a sweet spot for you. Using this feature allows you to post the location of your business.
- *Managing Multiple Instagram Accounts* — Starting in 2016, Instagram allows users to switch between multiple accounts from within the application.
- *Activity Status Tracker* — This feature allows users to know if their contacts are active. This

activity status can be seen from the direct message page, too.

- *Instagram TV* — This allows for longer videos. Users can share videos that are longer than 60 seconds, similar to TV episodes.
- *Hyperlink Username and Hashtags in Your Bio* — This is a bonus for you as a business person because it lets you engage with other accounts you have or the branded hashtags that your company uses.
- *Turn Existing Posts into Ads* — This feature isn't challenging to set up like some of the others; turn your organic posts into ads in the Ad Manager.
- *Emoji Slider Polls* — You can use emojis to poll how much users like or dislike an article. Marketers can use this feature to determine whether people love their products or not, and users can rate your favorite posts.

With Instagram, you can keep up with consumer demands and competition from other platforms. You already know that you have to keep up with new updates since new features can be added every time.

Aren't you thrilled with these excellent features? Well, as a potential marketer on this platform, wouldn't it be cool to check out the best and most high-profile social media content to post on Instagram? Let's check it out right now!

8.2 What Social Media Content to Post on Instagram

Instagram is a gold mine for your business. However, how do you showcase your expertise level, and display actions that bring you above some of the less inviting business posts that flood Instagram today?

Here, we reveal some of the most engaging types of brand posts on Instagram; they are sources of inspiration!

- *Giveaway Contests* — Try this. Ask ten people you know, or even ten random folks, whether they like free stuff. You might be surprised that 9 out of 10 will say yes. Now, this is interesting; these people dominate Instagram. With the mindset that everyone wants freebies, you can turn to contests and giveaways to help you get rapid and impressive responses. It is also a sure way to grow the size of your audience, and attract some attention to your products and services. To entice customers, use this means to create a desire for your products.

- *Thought Leadership* — When you think of a visual presentation of your products, think Instagram. But is it just about snapping pictures of the product? Definitely not! You have to put more perfection into your visual language so that you can get the followers you want. Ensure that your post features core competency to set your brand apart from others. To help you excel and display excellent thought leadership, embrace the use of a unique selling point (USP) for your business products and service.

- *Celebrity and Influencer Endorsement* — If you run a business that is more specialized for a specific audience, say, for example, professional athletes, then when you incorporate an influencer, you are likely to be rated for credibility and higher reach. Nike is a perfect example of this. When they wanted to introduce the pro-hijab design, they excellently used an image of Zeina Nassar and other influencers to send the message to users. Many users liked it, and more than 300,000 liked the picture. You can tap into this pattern; use influencers and celebrities to skyrocket your product acceptance and broaden your reach.

- *Holidays and Events* — You can boost your brand by publishing holiday-themed content on Instagram. Keep essential holidays and special events in mind. Surprisingly, during these times, you can cap peak sales and get a more significant portion of revenue. However, you first have to get through to your target audience and figure out which of the holidays are important to them. You can learn from what Disney did recently, and it set a beautiful example for startups. They subtly convince their target audience that the holidays aren't complete without them. Can you go beyond some of the more important holidays? Absolutely! As a brand, you can also tap into the quirky social media holidays to get more engagement. Why is this idea useful? There are wide gaps between these major holidays; if you can incorporate social media holidays into your brand, you will have many holidays and events to style into your business. On top of that, these could also serve as conversation starters.

- *Memes* — Yes, these are useful posts to utilize on Facebook; Instagram uses this format, too. Your brand can specialize in creating memes that people can relate to. Barkbox used this, and they got excellent results. With 1.5 million followers, Barkbox created memes that dog-owners would find relatable. While this can be accomplished when there isn't any holiday in sight, you can spice your game up by incorporating this during holiday seasons. You can double your audience interaction by making use of a style that is perfect for you.

- *Product Launches* — Ideally, you might think to use this pattern as a post on your Instagram business account. Well, that's a nice move if you did think that way. When doing this, ensure that you craft a product-focused message. That way, you can draw attention to new products and launches in a professional way. You can either be direct or subtle. When Qatar Airways introduced a new product design, they weren't overt about it; all they did was post the image of the original design and roll their standard text. However, they encouraged to focus on the tiny details in the picture that would ease the trip. They accomplished a product launch yet remained subtle. You could tap into this style once in a while.

- *Popular Hashtags* — There are even more things you can post on your Instagram page, but you have to search through a gold mine. Be smart in scouting for these hashtags. To achieve this, keep your eye on trending hashtags. Design a way to build these hashtags around your business to get the response that will encourage prospective customers to purchase your products.

- *Behind the Scenes* — Before you establish your brand, you'll probably want a sneak peek into how significant companies go about their daily activities and build up their products. Many people appreciate that but don't overdo it. Learn from Dior. In one if its engaging posts, Dior showed an atelier that was preparing Alana Haim's dress for an event. Most brands will not reveal everything about their companies, but showing some aspects is important and brings them closer to their audience. Additionally, if you intend to carry this out, it works better when it is planned around significant shows. Learn how to carry this out expertly.

- *Employee- and Workplace-Related* — Another excellent post to try out on Instagram is sharing pictures of your employees. When a brand does this, its consumers are informed that they have transparency, improving how their business is perceived. Would you assemble your employees and snap and share their pictures? You could, but it doesn't show professionalism. Do this when your employees are attending a significant event like volunteering work or community development work. When you share this, you remind your consumers of your company's traits and values.

When an audience sees faces that make the brand soar, they are impressed and want to commit to the brand.

- *Artsy Stuff* — Here is another excellent type of post for your Instagram feed. You can implement doodles, calligraphy, and sketches to boost your audience's interest. If your business brand centers around that, take advantage of the style and pattern and up your skill. You can also decide to use fan art and showcase it on your page. Sharing your talents online brings your expertise to light, and people will undoubtedly be amazed at your level of execution. Just ensure that you show consideration as you reveal those images, and don't forget to include an eye-catching and complementary caption to neatly key in your message.

- *Testimonials* — Testimonials work great on Facebook, and you can adopt the same technique on Instagram. You'll recall that the primary motive of using this medium is to ensure that you show the world what customers are saying about your business. You'll let the world see how genuine and impressive your services are. Also, apart from using these to showcase how you get things done, you can use testimonials to show potential customers how your current consumers use your product. Don't rely on quotes; go more in-depth by sharing visuals. Keep your customers' pictures and comments when they have business dealings with you. These archives are valuable in the future for decent and substantial promotion of your brand.

- *Throwbacks* — You probably know what this means, but if not, don't worry. Using throwback posts is an excellent way for brands to increase sales. If your business has been in the industry for quite a long time, do you have a post to share that will reveal your rich heritage or your legacy? Be sure to add or share only high-quality videos or pictures of a significant event that has been posted before. You can see how imperative it is to have an archive where important details are kept.

- *Transformation Pictures* — It is likely that you aren't as familiar with this due to it being less popular. However, you can stylishly incorporate it into your brand. Has your company shifted from an old-fashioned method of handling a task to something more advanced and modern? Share a picture or video that reveals how you've harnessed technology or other innovations in giving consumers the best output. When you do, the audience will be thrilled and will be convinced that you are committed to serving them. Doing so also puts you at a stage where you are considered relevant in your industry.

- *Product Features* — If you want to create a following around your product, then Instagram has you covered. Some brands excel with the use of this style. You will always see their products at the center stage. Adapting this style into your brand lets you reveal the values that your brand keeps up with, impressively skyrocketing your uniqueness. To do this, think about the value that your brand stands for, or what you uphold. If your audience appreciates such style or organization, then feature that in one of your designs or products. You are creatively unveiling some of your values, which will improve your sales.

- *Do It Yourself Ideas* — Interactions between consumers and producers aren't limited to asking questions and getting instant feedback. It goes beyond that, and one of the ways to establish this relationship is by developing DIY ideas. Your brand can research a product and design something simple that centers around what your brand stands for. Then, give your audience an idea of how they can create it. This pattern elevates your posts from boring content that is only about your products and reveals creativity through listening to your audience's interests.

- *Hyperlapse Videos* — At this point, you've figured out that visual elements are the key to Instagram. Hyperlapse videos showcase these gems in this social network app. The function of hyperlapse videos is to place a brand in a position where they can employ a fresh spin on mundane images. You give your audience a brief glimpse of what you have in your warehouse. More importantly, it can be incorporated into a behind the scenes video.

- *Post Statistics and Numbers* — You can't completely rule out the power of stats and numbers. Even though the power lies in visual images and videos, posting stats and numbers is also a strong point. All you have to do is transform some dull figures into appealing numbers that tell stories. If your brand has a report that comes with excellent stats, don't hesitate to use it in telling inspiring visual stories.

- *Offers and Promotions* — You've probably been waiting for this part. Similar to the freebies highlighted earlier, everyone loves offers. Luckily, you aren't willing to trade good sales. Even though you can't add a link to your business page, you can still master the dramatic art of creativity by using this type of post. Use your position to build healthy relationships between you and your consumers by posting about your sales and offers. These will serve as reminders that your audience shouldn't miss out on your deals.

- *Direct Readers to Your Blog* — How do you accomplish this when there isn't a way to add links to your Instagram page? Don't worry; you can make this work. Let's say you have a deal on your blog, or you've written sizzling and high-quality content. You can cleverly ask readers to check out the idea online by visiting your blog or website!

Isn't this list exhaustive? Before we wrap up this chapter, we need to discuss one aspect of ads on Instagram - photo ads. These are highly efficient, and top brands have never ignored them. Let's take a look at these in the next section.

8.3 How to Create a Photo Ad on Instagram

Some individuals use sponsored posts as ads on Instagram. They negotiate with an influencer on Instagram and ask them to help promote their products and services.

Unfortunately, this has limitations, and some of it

involves cost. Dealing with an influencer demand that you reach out and carry out negotiations, and there is no recourse if the influencer fails to deliver. Although utilizing sponsored posts today still holds relevance, there are several other opportunities advertisers can take advantage of.

By the start of 2015, anyone could master the process of creating ads through the Facebook self-service advertising section. This capability allows you to be in total control of who sees the ads and how they appear. Using this means instead of a sponsored post gives you reasonable pricing, self-service, immediate use, high reach, and refined audience targeting. Well, there are also several types of Instagram ads, including photo ads, video ads, stories ads, carousel ads, and slideshow ads.

Even though there are several ways to create ads on Instagram, this section only highlights the "photo ads" feature. A photo ad is a simple photo positioned in either a landscape or a square format. If you want the most straightforward visual ads, photo ads are the best option. Before we continue to the step-by-step guide, here are a few reminders:

- First, if you want to connect to your Instagram account, you can add it through your business manager on Facebook, or connect through your page's settings.
- Second, prepare whatever images and videos you want to use for your ads.
- Third, be sure to validate the type of Facebook advertising objectives that align with your marketing goal. With these fundamental principles at heart, you can start the process of creating Instagram photo ads.

Step 1: *Link Instagram Account to Facebook Page* — You need to link your Instagram account to your Facebook account. Move to the settings for your Facebook page and click on "Instagram Ads." Log in with your Instagram login credentials. If you don't already have an Instagram account, make one.

Step 2: *Create an Instagram Ad Campaign* — Move to the Ads Manager and create your first campaign. On the Ads Manager page, select "Campaigns," then click "Create."

Step 3: *Select Objectives for Ad Placement* — Choose the objective that matches and supports Instagram as an ad placement. After selection, click "Continue."

Step 4: *Get Your Ad Set Ready* — Now is the time to input your details. These details include the information for your ad set. Here, you can choose "Purchase" as the type of conversion you for which you want to optimize. You can turn on "Offer," so you get more conversion on your ad. Decide the privacy setting, such as who you want to see your ads, and set your budget. If you've gone through this before on Facebook, you won't have much trouble because this is similar.

Step 5: *Select Ad Placement* — You'd notice that, at the placement section, you can choose "Edit Placement." At this point, select "Instagram", so your ads appear on Instagram. If you select Instagram, your ads will run correctly on Instagram, but if you choose "Automatic," your ads will run across a variety of Facebook placements, including Instagram, and this gives you the best value. When you are done, select "Continue."

Step 6: *Add Details* — It is time to add a few details for your ad links, identity, and formats.

Step 7: *Preview* — After these details have been filled out, select "Preview" to check your ads before you submit them for review.

Step 8: *Wait for Approval* — Once approved, your ads will be displayed on Instagram.

Your Quick Start Action Step:

Did you know that most people don't apply the practical and simplified things they read? One reason is due to the lack of guides or detailed step-by-step to guide them. Therefore, we're going to provide you with all the means necessary to practically implement this knowledge:

1. *Locate where your target audience resides. This could take a week or more but don't worry; it's worth the search.*
2. *Spend the next two weeks posting non-paid advertisements. During these weeks, give your audience the best videos and posts on Instagram.*
3. *Offer discounts and promotions the following week. As soon as you get a larger audience, start creating paid ads.*
4. *Use a full week to design your paid ads. Ask for advice from leading companies, and do in-*

depth research on the content you want to use. If it takes you more weeks, don't be worried; you want to provide the best.

5. *Create an account in preparation for the paid ads. Apply all the steps discussed.*

6. *Create ads when you want peak sales, but don't stop using traditional posts weekly or monthly.*

Chapter 9:
Using YouTube

Chapter 9: Using YouTube

9.1 Definition of YouTube

While you probably know what YouTube is, you may not have heard about some of its most significant aspects — its marketing potential being only one of them.

YouTube is a website designed for and dedicated to sharing videos. Users all over the world with Internet connectivity can create accounts on the site with their email address, and upload videos that can be watched by anyone interested.

One of the reasons why YouTube is so impressive is its inception. People who are interested in sending large files to anyone that demands them can't send them via email. However, when YouTube became the focus of public attention, many who wanted to send large files could post a video on YouTube. After that, the URL of the video could be sent to whomever. This process provides us with one of the fundamental reasons why YouTube was established — posting and sharing videos.

Since then, YouTube has widely been used by brands as an excellent marketing tool. In fact, with a viral video—a video that has been liked and shared to a considerable degree—brands can wittingly reach their fullest potential. Thus, business owners should tap into this opportunity to reach their potential consumers by creating a YouTube account for marketing through video ads.

If you're delighted by this opportunity available to you, you no doubt want to know some of its features. Here, we'll highlight some of the key features and explain the benefits surrounding their use:

- *Live Streaming* — This feature was made available by YouTube in 2013 after a few years of operation. Today, only a few people are making use of this feature. Many have shifted to Periscope, the live streaming video app on Twitter. However, you have a wide door of opportunity open to you. To use the YouTube Live Stream feature, you must have at least 1,000 subscribers. So, if you have this opportunity, it shows that you've got a solid ground. Be careful when using this feature because you can't edit whatever you've released; it's essential to be prepared.

- *Fan Finder* — The YouTube fan finder is excellent and straightforward. It finds a potential fan and shows your channel ad to them in the form of a skippable TrueView Ad. Amazingly, it comes with no cost to you. Simply put, this feature allows people to know you and love your channel. To use this, upload a channel ad like an ordinary video, then move ahead to submit it for full review through the Fan Finder page.

- *Captioning* — This feature helps YouTube users discover your video. All you need to do is add English subtitles. It was found that adding English Language subtitles can increase views by 4%. Additionally, captioning can improve how you are seen on the search engine, as it allows your video to rank higher. As a marketer, learn to use this captioning well.

- *Embedding Features* — How do you think it will feel when your video is embedded in an article you're reading to illustrate the topic further? Isn't that a great stamp of approval? If you agree, then always enable embedding for all videos that you publish. To do that, go to the video manager, click on edit on the video, then move to advance settings and click on embed. The more you allow video embedding, the more you expand your viewers.

- *360 Degree Videos* — This feature allows users to see what's happening at any given location. Interestingly, this feature is made available on almost all mobile devices. Drone-based recording and video capturing are increasingly gaining popularity. Therefore, there is no denying that the 360-degree feature of YouTube allows you, as a marketer, to provide exciting and detailed content to viewers.

- *Subscriber Notifications* — This fantastic feature lets fans know whenever there is an update on a new video. Thus, by using this feature, your subscribers won't have a fear of missing out. Whenever you publish a new video, they'll be in the know; they get a notification through email and mobile, which is a soothing relief for you.

Well, with all these features, let's see what video posts you can accomplish!

9.2 What Videos to Post on YouTube

Did you know that YouTube has more than a billion users globally? Amazing, right? This signals a fantastic opportunity for you. However, you can't take advantage of it without a YouTube channel, particularly one that you are intent on utilizing for efficient marketing.

One of the questions that bother most YouTube users today is which YouTube video ideas should be posted on YouTube since there is a vast number of topics to choose from. Deciding on which plan to implement can be daunting. But don't worry! You're ahead of the game, and we've got you covered!

Listed below are incredible, startling video ideas that marketers can give their audience to market their brand awesomely. Now that you are ready, let's take a look:

- *Make Your Intention Known for Loved Gadgets* — You should be cautious about this. If your brand is centered around gadgets, then use your videos to show off new devices or tweaks that you've added to your gadgets. Talk about your love for these gadgets.

- *Dig Deeper into Tech Discussions* — Do you find that many people have difficulty understanding technological concepts? Why not use this option to give some detailed explanations? But be careful to avoid being too fluffy. Make sure you do your research and come up with a comprehensive statement that is straightforward to understand. Just be sure to breakdown the intricate parts; you'll be surprised at how eager your viewers will be for updates.

- *Be in on the Gossip* — Do it reasonably and know what you are saying. Is there a new product that is being criticized or exonerated? Now is the time to make your research count and come up with an intensive explanation. You aren't only joining the conversation; you are showing your strength in regards to your exposure and brand credibility.

- *Show off Company's New Acquisition* — Is there a new device your brand has acquired to foster excellent delivery to consumers and prospects? You can use your video to reveal an inside story, and what you hope to accomplish with the new tool. This way, your viewers are sure that you have their best interests at heart.

- *Play Games with Other Channels* — You can make your YouTube channel more collaborative. Use your videos to reveal how you play games with other channels, and make sure that you strategically use that to inform your viewers about what your brand stands for.

- *Show Creative Ways of Recycling* — If your brand has a connection with sustainability, you can give and teach lessons on recycling. For example, show them the best way they can recycle an item. Tactfully, you can carry out recycling work in your company and, after that, share how you did it and how others can get do it, too.

- *Give Financial Planning Tips* — When people see that you are interested in their welfare, they will commit to your brand. If you are finding it challenging to identify where you are to start, give this a try. Advise people who might be searching for financial tips. You can dive into topics like stocks, savings, and bonds.

- *Create an Ad* — Ads aren't expensive, which we'll discuss further in the next section. Therefore, don't hesitate to give them a shot. Create an ad and flaunt what your brand is aiming at. Monitor every stage of the advertisement, and edit, edit, edit before you finally publish. Ensure that the message isn't confusing to understand, so a wide range of viewers can interpret it.

- *Give Job Placement Advice* — If your brand preparing for a massive or small-scale recruit, expand your reach by showing your viewers a few dos and don'ts. You are already aware that this stage can be daunting and crazy. When you help them out with these demanding tasks, they will gain interest in your brand, and if they aren't chosen, they'll still see your company as being honest and transparent.

- *How-to Videos* — These can be similar to DIY tools. Is there something your fans know that you can do? Show them how to do it! That's what they're interested in, so make sure that you provide.

- *Give Detailed Processes* — We love ease, and your audience loves that, too. The desire for users to learn more about a subject matter can be illustrated best on YouTube. Break down the complicated stuff and explain it.

- *Share Fun Facts* — You don't have to be all business all the time. It is excellent to enforce fun in your brand marketing. In the world of YouTube videos, you can't write this off. Just go in-depth on things that many are oblivious to and bring out the fun. Always work to stay relevant.

- *Tap into Science* — Does your brand relate to science? Explain some of the natural world ideas and see how it matches up with science to give your product a boost.

- *Upload a Short Comedy* — The basic concept of this comedy is to teach the audience the value of your product. Just find what many people are talking about, and use comedy to show what your product will do to solve the problem. Be sure that it is funny, and don't let it transcend the overall lesson you want to teach; find a happy medium.

- *Discuss and Illustrate Time Management Tips* — More than 90% of people would love to have more hours added to their day. Unfortunately, that can't be done. However, you can use your brand to teach others how time can be managed well. This approach instills good traits that your company upholds, and people will be convinced that, by partnering with you, they won't be wasting their precious time. As a bonus, they learn a lesson about time management.

- *Show Love to the Environment* — Regardless of your brand, you have to be eco-friendly. In developed lands, government officials have been advising consumers to discontinue from companies or brands that have failed to embrace the act of limiting their carbon footprints. Is your company intent on reducing its carbon footprint? Show the world how exemplary you are. Your subscribers should know that you aren't raining havoc on the ecosystem while selling your products and services. Instead, you are selling your brand while taking care of the planet.

- *Give Advice on Styling* — If your brand is centered around fashion, then show your brilliance and tell your audience what they want to hear, as long as it is something practical and reliable. Give guidance about fashion and styling to your viewers. Reveal your opinions and insights in your YouTube videos. Just make sure to be bold and confident.

- *Give Tutorials* — Giving tutorials can reinforce connection and commitment. Who wants to spend hours on their makeup each morning when there is a more efficient way? Therefore, give your folks quick, at-home tutorials on how to accomplish that. At the same time, reveal your products and see if your viewers are interested in buying.

- *Organize an Amazing Song for Customers* — Consumers want brands that care for them. So, during holiday seasons, organize your employees and sing a heartwarming and fantastic song for your audience and buyers. If composing a new song isn't what your brand stands for, then find a song and track that has gained popularity, and sing it via your YouTube video. You will be amazed at how many viewers you pull in.

- *Cover a Big Event* — Is your brand invited to an event, or were you granted permission to attend? Cover the event and show what your employees accomplished while you were there. Make sure the event is in connection with your field or niche. Keep an eye on a big event, be present, and show your consumers. It works like magic!

9.3 How to Create a Video Ad on YouTube

Did you know that the best way to catch customers' attention is through visual aids? YouTube has existed for some time now, and with each passing minute, hours of videos are posted online. You may think this is a phase that will soon pass, but trust me, it will only get better from here.

Do you have goods and services to advertise? Do you

need a bigger and better audience? If you answered yes to one or both questions, then YouTube is the key to that advertisement success. As a YouTube user, you may have noticed that, before your video starts playing, some ad videos pop up first for a few seconds with the option to skip after a few minutes. This is the type of ad you will be creating.

You know that, once it's out, viewers won't have a choice but to watch what you are delivering to them. In this section, we will be detailing easy steps that will make it easier for you to create your successful advertisement on YouTube. Patiently follow as we go step by step through the secrets of YouTube Advertisement.

Step 1: *Create a Google AdWords Account* — You need a Google AdWords account to start. This is the first step to take on your quest to create an advertisement on YouTube. Once you have done that, then you need to proceed to the "Create a new video" section. Go to www.adwords.google.com to start your campaign and create your video. This step will push you into the spotlight and kickstart your YouTube video creation.

Step 2: *Link AdWords to Your YouTube Account* — Upon completing the creation of your AdWords account, the next step is to link your AdWords account with your YouTube account. This action will ensure that your campaign and ads are active. From your AdWords account, find the navigation menu and click on "Linked YouTube Accounts." If you don't link the two accounts together, your ads will not be made available on YouTube, so this is an essential step you must take. Linking is easy as long as you already have a YouTube account, and keep in mind that the same Google account will power both accounts.

Step 3: *General Settings* — The next step is controlling the activity of your ad. In the dashboard, go to the General Settings. In the General Settings, you will be required to set the expected or desired budget for each day. It is advisable to start small and slowly increase as you get more familiar with the system and form a more defined objective. A typical spend is around $0.1 - $0.23. It's also good to know that you won't be paying Google unless people are viewing your ads all the way through. Other customization options are available for bidding for advanced advertisers.

Step 4: *Set the Location Where Your Ad Will Be Displayed* — Your ad won't just be flying aimlessly across YouTube; you have an option to choose the countries, regions, cities, ZIP codes, and IP addresses that will have access to your advertisement, among other criteria. You can go as broad as you want to reach a wider audience, but you can also be specific if your audience is identifiable. If you are specific to your audience, then your viewer will be more qualified for your ads. If you are interested in building general brand awareness for your industry or your products, then it is advised to go a little broader.

Step 5: *Upload Your Video* — The next thing on the list is selecting the video you want to upload. You can drag and drop, or you can choose a file and then upload it to your account from YouTube. It is best to give your video the design that will make it the most captivating and exciting for your viewers. Before uploading your video, there are some essential things you should know, like the allowed format, and the way to give your video more success. You can access this online and decide before uploading your video.

Step 6: *Advanced Settings* — Click on the Advanced

Settings, and choose what day and time you want your ad to be displayed (you can be specific if you know the time and day your audience will be available, or when your prospective customers are more likely to view your ad). You can also assign the start and end day of your new advertisement. Another good option is to shut off your ad from 12 a.m. to 6 a.m. when most people are inactive. You can set the ad to run during lunchtime and leisure hours. In short, select the time when you know your prospective customers will be available to watch your YouTube ad.

Step 7: *Move to Device Targeting* — Device targeting is another brilliant step that will make your video advertisement more successful. Device targeting will make it easier to select targeted devices like mobile, desktop, laptop, tablets, and more. This step is advantageous when you know precisely the type of device your customer will be making use of. Are your customers on mobile phones? Is your ad for a mobile app? Then select the mobile option.

Step 8: *Select Age, Gender, Topic, and More* — Not all content will be appropriate for every audience. YouTube is filled with categories of users who may find your ad inappropriate or unhelpful. This step will help you select the age and gender of viewers you want to target and help you specify which topic you will be displaying. When you are specific, there are higher chances of hitting the right audience. There are categories, interests, words, websites, and phrases you may want to show your audience. Hence, you need to be specific about your target audience to help get the information to them. Imagine creating an ad about games, videos, or apps for teens. If only adults age 50 and older see the video, then you have failed to reach your audience. Hence, you need to be more specific about your audience.

Step 9: *Choose Keywords* — It is crucial to search for specific keywords to help you get to the right audience. You should be able to identify the keywords your potential customers will be targeting and searching for on YouTube. You can make use of the Google Keyword Tools to search for the relevant keywords in the field of your choice, and the specific terms you may use. The terms you will be using are selected from Google's search engine, not YouTube. However, even with this, they are useful for weeding out the inappropriate and ineffective words, leaving you with the best keywords. Beyond this, it will ensure that only the right people view your ads. When your keyword is long, and when it is specific to your audience, then it will be more beneficial for your business. It will help you capture the right group of people, which is your original purpose.

These nine steps are the basis for starting your YouTube advertisements. This list is a taste of all of the available information for beginners who are interested in advertising with YouTube.

If you follow the steps identified and provided in this guide, it will be easier for you to create and direct the best YouTube video ads possible.

Your Quick Start Action Step:

Generally speaking, if you know what you want to accomplish in six months, start it now! In saying that, we'll help out with some quick start action steps so that you can get the best results:

1. *Spend a week writing down who your target audience is, and pick the five best video ideas among those that have been highlighted above.*

2. *Spend a week crafting excellent content that will meet your target audience. If you aren't done in a week, don't rush. Give yourself time. Spending quality time is better than showing irrelevant and mediocre ads.*

3. *Think about how much you can afford, how much you want to budget, and how long you want the ads to run.*

4. *Decide whether you will use one video per week or two videos per week.*

5. *Note your track record. How is your ad faring? Excellently? If not, then check what could be wrong and avoid making the same mistake on the next post.*

6. *Offer promos and giveaway content to widen your brand's reach.*

7. *For the first five months, check your progress and see how you've fared compared to when you weren't utilizing ads or posts on the website. No doubt, you will see a positive difference.*

Chapter 10:
Using Twitter

Chapter 10: Using Twitter

10.1 Definition of Twitter

The next social media platform that you can effectively use to increase awareness about your product online is Twitter. Before going into detail, let's define this social media platform for the benefit of those that are not familiar with it.

Twitter is a free social media networking platform where users can share messages, known as "tweets," to other users on the platform.

With millions of active daily users, the Twitter platform is quickly becoming one of the most effective social media platforms. In comparing Twitter with other popular social media platforms, Margaret Rouse noted that, unlike with Facebook and LinkedIn, you do not need to be friends with or accepted by a user to get notifications of their posts on Twitter (Rouse, What Is Twitter?).

You can post text, images, and videos on Twitter to your followers, but the content is limited to just 140 characters. However, with only these short messages, your tweets can reach up to millions of people using the tools and features available on this platform.

What are some of the helpful features for your business on the Twitter platform? Twitter is unique and different from other platforms, considering the way you send messages and how you reach out to people on this platform.

Twitter has some unique features which can be very helpful in your social media marketing strategies. Here we are going to look at the features that will be most helpful in your brand building and marketing strategy:

- *Twitter Ads* — The Twitter platform has its specific ads, just like Facebook, where you can reach out to your targeted audience to promote your brand and increase sales. Twitter ads have become popular, according to statistics, which show that ad engagement has increased by 63% since 2018, and cost per ad engagement has declined by 23% (Newberry, 2018). With Twitter ads, you can use data available on the platform to reach out to people who will be interested in your brand. You can promote a particular tweet, your account, and your brand using specific parameters that will enable you to target your audience. Whenever you see a tweet, trend or account tagged, promoted, and posted for people to notice, then you know that they are being promoted through Twitter ads.

- *Twitter List* — The Twitter list is one underrated Twitter tool that we seldom use, and it has the potential to improve your social media marketing strategies. With a Twitter list, you can follow tweets of some specific people or brands to ensure that you do not miss anything and keep up with the industry news. The Twitter list enables you to make a list of selected Twitter accounts where you can see all tweets related to those accounts. You can also make a list of people or brands of a specific industry, or people that always engage in particular topics. This strategy will enable you to improve engagement with these handles and stay up-to-date with happenings in the industry. You can keep up with your competition and engage the people who are interested in your brand. The Twitter list helps to improve brand engagement and increase awareness as you keep up-to-date with tweets of interest on this platform. You can make your list either public or private. You can also subscribe to a public listing or private list of people that are of interest to your brand.

- *Twitter Image Collage* — You can engage more people with tweets containing images, as it's known that tweets with images capture more attention. Twitter allows you to post pictures along with 140 characters to describe the photos. This feature is another way to catch the attention of your audience through the use of catchy and trendy images. Twitter allows you to post up to four images in a collage form, but you cannot caption each image, unlike what you can do on Facebook. You will have to write a description that suits the pictures you posted in a collage format. Twitter collage allows you to promote your brand using a variety of images related to your business. The images should be clear, the right size, and relevant to your business.

- *Videos and GIFs on Twitter* — One of the best ways to boost business is through virtual presentations using videos and GIFs. Posting videos related to your business will increase engagement and promote business awareness. As a brand, you can make videos describing your brands and their services. Also, you can quickly share how to use your products or services, which will engage your audience based on their interests.

- *Featured Tweets* — Tweets are used to promote your brand and business as you share content related to your business with your audience. The people who check out your tweets will usually check your profile and your previous tweets as well to learn more about your brand. When going through your tweets, users might not go through all of them, and may not reach some essential tweets if they are further down your timeline. You can use the Featured Tweets feature to promote relevant tweets for those who visit your profile. You can stamp a tweet at the top of your timeline, so it will be the first tweet anyone sees when they visit your profile. This feature enables you to promote your best tweet to engage your audience more.

- *Twitter Dashboard* — The Twitter dashboard

is another critical feature that can be used to promote your brand. With your Twitter account registered, you will edit your profile and place your logo on your dashboard, and other related business on your profile. With this, anybody that searches on your Twitter profile will get useful information about your business, promote your business, and create awareness.

10.2 What Social Media Posts to Tweet on Twitter

Twitter is a unique platform, and if you want to make an impact with your tweets, they have to be engaging. You have to be creative with your tweets to encourage people to like or retweet them and gain more online readership.

We are going to share a few tips on how to make your tweets engaging and exciting to your audience, and get your tweets viral.

Here are some tips to help you trend on Twitter:

- Your tweet should be innovative and interesting to encourage people to share it. The more that people retweet your tweets, the more you are advertising your brand to more people, and you can even go viral. Make the facts more interesting to catch the attention of your audience. Then they will share the tweets with others and increase your chances of going viral.

- The hashtag is one of the most essential tools to increase engagement on Twitter. Twitter is made up of millions of people, and it is impossible to reach all those who are interested in what you are tweeting about. With the use of hashtags, which have the "#" symbol placed in front of a keyword relating to the topic, those who are searching for the topic can easily see it when they search for it on Twitter. It has been found that the use of hashtags increases engagement by 100% (Cuninghame, 2019).

- Twitter users are aware of trending topics, which you can find on your Twitter platform. These trending topics represent the most popular and most discussed topics on Twitter. You can be a part of these conversations by using the hashtags with the keywords that are trending. People following that topic will be able to see your tweet on this real-time discussion. This is how your tweets can become trending as you join popular discussions on this platform. One trick you should use is to ensure that the trending topics you utilize are related to your brand, so you can target audiences who will be interested in your tweet.

- Making your tweet more personal rather than formal will increase engagement and make people retweet the post. Twitter is an engaging platform that encourages less formal conversation, so you can get more people to like your tweet by getting more personal. You can promote your tweet in a story format in what we refer to as a "thread." This thread engages the audience as they follow the story to the end, and they'll share it by retweeting it to their followers as it gets more responses.

- You can ask your followers for a retweet if they are loyal to you, and they enjoy your tweets and your brand. You should make sure to ask them to retweet a critical tweet, and don't overuse this privilege. They will get tired of retweeting your tweets if you ask them to retweet every time. This is an old-fashioned way of getting a retweet, and you should do it if you have a substantial number of followers who will create a buzz online.

- You are going to create less buzz on Twitter if you post at the wrong time, even if your post is more engaging and you expect a considerable number of retweets. Posting at a time when your followers are less active online will result in less response than anticipated. Determine when a large number of your followers are active online and post at that time, increasing the chances of your post going viral. Do research on the best time to post and the time of the day when most of your audience will be online.

10.3 How to Create an Ad on Twitter:

To create an ad on Twitter, you first have to have a registered account with the platform. Once that first, necessary task is complete, follow the steps below to create your ad:

Step 1: The first thing you have to do in creating an ad for Twitter is log in to the desired account that you want to use on the campaign. You cannot promote your brand or business through another person's account. When you log in to your account, you can move to the next step in creating an ad on Twitter.

Step 2: The next step is to go to "Ads" on Twitter, which you can find on the platform. This step is another easy way to direct the user to the Ads section on Twitter.

Step 3: After going to the section for Twitter ads, you will be asked to choose between promotional tweets or Twitter ads. Promotional tweets are used to promote a particular tweet to a broader range of people, including your followers and those who do not follow you. The tweet you are promoting should contain links to your business and crucial information to increase awareness about the company. The other option you can choose from is the Twitter ads promotion campaign to increase followers and engagement on the platform. The Twitter ads will give suggestions to other Twitter users on who to follow as they appear on their Twitter timeline.

Step 4: The next step is to choose the objective for your Twitter ads. From this, you will understand that promotional tweets are more direct than Twitter ads. The eight goals you will select from in this section include app installs, followers, tweet engagement, promoted video views, website clicks or conversion, app re-engagement, stream video views, and awareness. On the other hand, ad campaigns are focused more on promoting the Twitter account to gain followers as you expose the brand.

Step 5: At this stage, we are more focused on filling in the details of the campaign to guide it to the desired audience from start to finish. This is when you will fill in the details that will direct and guide the Twitter ad campaign. These include: when the campaign begins and ends, the categories of people to target, your budget, and other details that may pop up depending on the type of campaign. You fill in the form that appears after you decide which kind of campaign you want to pursue.

Step 6: In this step, you have to create an ad group, which will be a follow-up to the bigger ad group on the left-hand side. The new group you want to create will now appear on the right-hand side as a subgroup to the larger group with a higher budget. These will run for a longer time than the main group.

Step 7: After the successful creation of the group and subgroup, you will now move to select the audiences you want to target in each group. The larger group and subgroup will target particular audiences that relate to the criteria in each group, depending on their age, location, culture, interests, gender, and other criteria that will increase the chances of engagement.

Step 8: Select how you want these tweets to be promoted, using available tweets or specific tweets that will further promote each group in this ad campaign.

Step 9: Go through all that you have done and chosen as you review the promotional guides and packages before launching the campaigns.

We have made it easy to launch your Twitter campaigns as you seek to engage more people and increase brand awareness. Twitter is one of the best platforms to run paid ads to reach out to more people. Twitter has the potential to expose your brand worldwide, so you should take note and be patient with the process.

There are so many articles online that are helpful and can be of use in promoting your business using the Twitter platform, but we recommend that you visit the link https://business.twitter.com/en.html for a quick guide through the process of running successful Twitter ads.

Your Quick Start Action Step:

Twitter ads are essential to a successful social media campaign, and you should be very careful in going through these steps. To quickly get started with your Twitter ad campaign, you should follow the action steps below:

1. *Create a series of engaging tweets with useful information about the brand, which is ready to be launched with the campaign.*
2. *The tweets you want to be promoted should be featured to appear at the top of your timeline with visual impressions, such as images and videos.*
3. *Retweet interesting tweets, comments that you are retweeted or mentioned in, and comments that engage your promotional tweets.*
4. *Get personal with your audience through your*

tweets, and engage your audience through your retweets.

Chapter 11:
Putting It All Together — How to Launch an Integrated Social Media Marketing Campaign

Chapter 11: Putting It All Together — How to Launch an Integrated Social Media Marketing Campaign

11.1 A Tactical Approach to Launching Your Campaign

Social media marketing is a comprehensive approach to promoting your brand and increasing sales, so it will require a tactical approach to get good results. Social media defines platforms that make up several channels with a massive number of followers reaching billions.

To approach the marketing campaign in a manner that will ensure you use your resources properly and effectively, you need to work with various social media platforms to achieve your aims and objectives.

As we have mentioned earlier, there are several social media platforms, and if you want to run campaigns on all of these platforms, you must dispatch a colossal amount of resources. You could hire social media managers with many workers to work on different platforms, but this will require a substantial amount of investment.

However, if you want to make an impact with your social media marketing campaign, you must be tactical in your approach. You must understand your target audience and know where you can reach out to these audiences. Each of these platforms is unique and can attract different categories of people. You must keep this in mind when you are selecting the platform you want to invest in social media marketing. You do not want to spend your resources reaching out to millions of people on social media platforms and not make any impact on your brand awareness or sales just because those millions you targeted were not interested in your brand.

This is what you will get when you go on a wild goose chase online with social media marketing; you make all the noise with no impact. Such efforts will result in total waste of time and resources. You will not have achieved your aim and objective in running the campaign on social media.

To achieve your objective, you have to understand your audience and where to find and approach them to be effective. This realization will require a thorough investigation of the kind of audience that will likely contact your brand, where they are likely to be located, and how to approach them when posting your content.

You will also have to research the various social media platforms and the kind of people you can find on these platforms. Will you be able to reach out to your targeted audience effectively on these platforms, and how are you going to approach these clients?

Understanding how to approach these platforms is another way you can effectively reach out to your target audiences. Some platforms are very business-friendly, and you have to be formal when approaching your audience. This is the case with business-friendly platforms like LinkedIn. LinkedIn is very different from personal platforms like Facebook and Twitter, where it is more beneficial to be informal in your approach. So, if you want a platform where you should be formal and business-like in your plan, then LinkedIn is your best choice.

However, some platforms, like Facebook and Twitter, are too popular to ignore, and you must include them in your social media marketing strategies. These platforms command billions of users, and you can approach all angles of social media marketing on these platforms.

Platforms like Facebook and Twitter are vast enough, and you can find all kinds of people through them. You can get to your targeted audience on these platforms by studying your target audiences and their behavior on these platforms. With these metrics, you can plan out strategies on how to approach them effectively and make a positive impact.

You can also find other platforms where you can approach a specific set of people, such as the famous, upcoming platforms like Snapchat and Pinterest. These tend to be the most popular with younger people, especially women. If your brands are geared toward women and younger people, then you can use these platforms to run your social media marketing campaign effectively.

In essence, if you want to run an effective, integrated social media marketing campaign, you have to understand the social media platforms that you want to use. The right combination of social media platforms that suits your marketing campaign will make it more useful for you to achieve your goals for your marketing strategies and campaigns.

11.2 Why You Need to Plan Your Social Media Marketing

Planning your social media marketing campaigns is one of the essential steps in achieving success in your marketing campaign. A plan will include studying your potential audience and the best platform to approach these audiences. This research is the first stage of your social media plan, and this preliminary stage will involve researching your audience and the platforms that you will successfully use to approach these audiences.

When you are aware of the platforms that are suitable for your targeted audience, the next step is how you are going to market on these platforms. This step includes planning what kind of posts are appropriate to promote your social media platform, and how you are going to get content to promote your brand. You will have to plan, research, and promote this content.

Planning the content requires that you stay consistent with your brand and style, as well as maintaining a regular posting schedule and keeping your audience engaged. Your marketing campaign should be well-planned, so you remain consistent with the kind of content you dish out to your audience.

To be consistent with the amount of content you send out weekly, you have to plan it to keep your audience engaged. You need to be predictable when you post your content, so your audience can rely on you. If you are inconsistent with the amount of content, and you don't deliver at a set time, you might lose your audience to a more reliable platform. Your audience may see you as an unreliable brand when you don't post content for long intervals, such as months apart.

For you to be consistent, a good plan on posting will have you try to meet each deadline to drop a new quality post. Without this idea, you will not feel obligated to match the number of posts you should be putting out weekly. An insight on when to post and what content to post will help you stay consistent and keep your audience engaged.

Draw out a plan to interact with your audience and keep them responsive. Have an idea of when to be online to engage customers by replying to their comments and opening up discussions. With this plan, you can research when to be online at the time your audience is most active. Without a well-laid plan, you will not be able to reach out to your targeted audience effectively, and in so doing, fall short in your engagement with your audience. This will ultimately affect your marketing plan.

A well-laid plan for your social media campaign will enable you to follow a structured schedule, and you will be active at the right time on the platform. Draw out a plan today for when to post content and engage your audiences as you seek to improve your marketing strategies for your social media marketing campaign.

11.3 How to Launch Social Media Campaigns

Here we are going to go through the detailed steps that you should follow to accomplish a successful social media campaign. If you want to be successful in your campaign, you need to plot out a detailed plan and stick to it.

The plan will help you stay on track, be consistent, and engage your audience constructively through your integrated social media campaigns. The integrated social media campaigns imply that you are using two or more social media platforms to reach out to your targeted audience.

Now, we are going to make it easy as we provide you with detailed steps that will ensure you are successful in your social media campaigns.

Step 1: *Know Your Social Status* — The first step is approaching your social media marketing campaign by first knowing your social status. This social status has to do with the value you have online and how effective your present state can help you improve your social media status.

The first thing to do is make a list of all the social media platforms you are engaged in and check your engagement status. Through this process, you make a list of the number of followers you have on each of platforms, how much engagement your posts have on these networks in terms of comments, and the performance of each platform based on the number of leads and sales each had.

You must first know yourself to make plans for the next steps and improve your status on these platforms. One of the reasons for analyzing your presence on these social media platforms is to ascertain which one is most suitable for you and your campaign.

You will end up knowing more about which platform you should continue with and which other platforms you can add to your social media campaigns. In the quest to improve your social media campaigns, you should analyze how you are going to introduce a broader audience to your platforms in terms of response, and increase leads.

For example, when using Facebook, you will analyze how your brand has been faring on the platform with its campaign. How many likes do you have on your Faccbook page, and how does your audience engage on your Facebook page? You should analyze how the people on your platform engage with and respond to you. You may have a good number of followers, but only have a small percentage that comment or share your posts. It may be because a higher percentage of these people are not interested in your brand. In knowing your status through this view, you will have to engage in social media campaigns to target people who want to be involved with your brand.

You can apply this to other social media platforms if you have enough followers but fewer responses in terms of lead generation and sale increase. At this stage, you should research your targeted audience and use the appropriate tools to target these audiences.

You should use Facebook ads and Twitter ads as the tools to target your specific audience. You will have the opportunity to direct your ads to a particular audience, which will, in turn, increase sales and leads for your brand. You do not have to spend much on these ads; you can budget any amount you choose for the campaign.

With these targeted ads, you can tailor your campaign to a specific category of people in order to stay within the amount budgeted for the project. The more you expand your target reach, the more you can spend on the ad campaign. If you are on a budget, you can reduce the number of people you target by selecting a group of people that will be interested in your brand and focusing on these specific categories of people.

Step 2: *Identify and Understand Your Target Audience* — Your target audience is the most critical aspect of your social media marketing campaign, and if you do not get it right with them, all of your efforts will be wasted. The next steps in guaranteeing a successful social media marketing campaign are getting to know your target audience and learning what they like and where you can meet them.

It is important to research who is likely to be interested in your brand, and once you can identify these groups of people, then you are halfway to your successful marketing campaign goal. These targeted audiences are the groups of people who are most likely to be interested in what you have to offer. Through isolating these groups, you can market to them online, and promote your brand to increase the probability of your succcss.

The first step is knowing who your target audience is and why these people are interested in your brand. You can research what kinds of people would be interested in your business, and also take a look at your competitors and their followers. This technique will enable you to understand which people you should target in your campaign to increase leads and sales.

Let's take a look at how to reach the targeted audience of a cosmetic brand. It makes sense that women are more likely to be interested in a cosmetic brand than men, and younger women are more likely to follow that brand on social media. With this simple analysis, in running this campaign, you would focus more on women than on men. When it comes to age branding, you will target a younger demographic who would find the brand more in tune with their style.

Still following the example we have stated above, we now have to focus on how to reach this target audience. We know that we are focusing on young women. Where can we find this group of people, and which platforms are best to reach out to them?

Facebook is the most popular social media platform, so we cannot ignore it and its massive number of active followers. Almost everyone is on Facebook, and that is a vast potential audience. If you have not already registered your business brand on Facebook, do that now and start engaging these people.

Through the use of Facebook ads, you can specify the types of people you want your campaign to reach, and reduce the amount of time you need to spend on the social platform. While setting the parameters, you can customize them to reach out to more women and younger ladies who would be interested in your brand, thus increasing awareness of the brand. Make sure your campaign is catchy and encourages your audience to take action through liking your page or visiting your website.

Take the time to research what interests people to increase the number of social media users visiting your page. Research the types of content that will be most appealing to your followers or friends on social media. You can also visit the pages of your competitors for a better idea on the topics that will help people develop an interest in your product, inspiring them to purchase it right away.

Step 3: *Your Aim and Objective* — Do not make the mistake of not having a goal or objective for your social media marketing campaign. What is the purpose of starting a marketing campaign on social media? Who is your target audience, and how are you going to get your message through to these people?

It would be a mistake to dive into social media and expect to successfully market your brand through random and aimless posting. You have to draw up a plan with a clear objective to your marketing on social media platforms.

Be specific about what you want to achieve on social

media, and how you intend to enact this plan. You may want to grow awareness about your brand by educating your followers about the importance of using certain items and other products, and the benefits of those items in the sale industry. Your aim may also be to increase sales and focus more on promoting products and services as you review products online.

Without a well-planned objective, you will end up randomly posting content online with no direction, and it will be difficult to measure your progress through these periods. However, when you have an objective planned out, you can measure your campaign's progress. If, for instance, you plan to increase sales, you can track how many items you've sold since you started the campaign, and compare that number to before you started the campaign to measure your success.

If creating awareness is the objective of your online campaign, then you can measure this by the number of people that have liked your page or posts, or by the number of people commenting on or sharing your content.

With an aim and objective, you have a direction on where your marketing is going. You can easily measure the success of your campaigns as you compare your current progress to your status before you started the campaigns; you'll be able to see how far you've come.

One thing you should understand is that people follow experts on social media, not brands that generally post about any topic. Once your brand becomes known for a particular thing, people become interested in your brand as an expert instead of as just another social media account.

Step 4: *Make a note of your progress* — What is the purpose of your social marketing campaigns if you do not measure your success to see how you are faring, and assure yourself that you are not wasting time and resources? How else will you be able to understand how you are doing if you do not check on your success matrix from time to time?

If you want to know how well your social media campaigns have been doing over time, you should look into the following:

- The conversion rate you have achieved over that period shows how many people have started following your brand, including the number of people that have bought items or services advertised on the platform since the start of your campaign.

- Check out the amount of time that people spend on your platform. If you keep dishing out exciting content, your audience will spend more time on your platform reading and sharing your content. On the other hand, users will skim and move on from content that they find less interesting and engaging; they'll spend less time on these platforms, thus reducing the engagement on the platform.

- Check out the number of people your content was able to reach out to. Once the campaign is doing well, you will see an increase in the number of people you've reached on the platform. This progress is a direct way to measure the reach of the content, as it crosses every demographic and boosts the potential of increasing sales and engagement.

- Find out the number of times your brand has

been mentioned on a platform. As your mentions increase, this is a sign that more people are talking about your products or brand. On platforms like Twitter, you will get notifications whenever people mention your brand name, so you can use this information to know how much your brand is being mentioned, and how well people are responding to it.

- Make a note of how often people share your content. Once people like what you are sharing with them, they will share this content with other people on that platform, and even on other platforms. Most of these platforms give you notifications when people share your content, so you can easily measure how your content is doing in terms of shares. If your shares are too low, then it is time to revise your plan and check out how to engage your audience more with better content that is posted at the right time.

Step 5: *Planning Your Content* — Content is key when it comes to social media marketing, and it is how you get to engage with the client regularly. You can do all the right things when it comes to creating your account up to your profile creation, but your social media marketing will be a total failure if you fail to engage your audience regularly with quality content.

Content involves posting articles, texts, images, videos, or GIFs that will engage your audience and encourage a response. Quality content should be part of your plan to promote your brand, engage your audience, and increase sales and leads. Good content is one of the surest ways of building trust and gaining authority on any platform.

There are different ways to post content that depends on the specific platforms and what you can post on these platforms. For example, Facebook is one of the few platforms where you can promote your brand through text posts, images, and videos, all on a single platform.

Twitter, on the other hand, seems to have evolved from a purely text-based platform. Now, the platform has introduced video sharing, which many brands have since used effectively to boost their marketing strategies. It is easy to post a link on Twitter, directing your audience to a post with the right text combined with the right visual.

Instagram is a platform that mainly utilizes image and video content to promote your brand, and it is the best platform for those brands that need to show quality images, such as fashion, food, or art, to showcase their products. Pinterest is another popular social media platform that makes use of images to promote products, as users share image content with each other.

There are other platforms like YouTube and Snapchat that make use of videos to promote brands and products. These platforms are very popular, and you can use a combination of any of these platforms in your social media marketing campaigns.

It would be a mistake to just jump into posting content without doing the proper research and planning that will guide you in your campaign. Before posting content, you should research the topic so that it will be catchy, and research keywords to use so your content can be easily found online.

It is also vital that you choose content that your audience is sure to find engaging and entertaining.

After you have found the right topic, you should then ensure that your content is original and contains accurate facts.

You should set up a schedule on when to post on your platform. With such a plan, you will maintain consistency and regularity with your posts.

Step 6: *Make Use of Social Media Tools* — In our present world, it has become easy to get tasks done quickly and efficiently through automation. Programmers have made processes easier, as they can come up with software to meet the needs of their clients.

With the help of these programmers, we now have tools that can automate some tasks for us online. Some tools can help you in your social media marketing strategies; they'll help you perform these tasks faster and more efficiently, even when you are not there to do them personally. One of our favorite tools is the one that automates your posts. With this tool, you can schedule a post to come online at a particular time, even if you are not online to do it yourself.

Using this tool, you won't miss out on posting content

at particular times you want to post, even if you are not available at that moment. This tool helps you keep up with posting for your clients at the scheduled times.

There are some other useful tools with different functions that can help you in your marketing strategies. Some tools will help you manage all the social media platforms you are using on one single platform. This tool will help you save time, as well as help you effectively handle all of your social media on a single account. With these tools, you can reply to your audience when they message you. You can also analyze all of the platforms you use for your social media campaigns and easily measure how your campaigns are doing.

There are so many tools available for you to use to manage your social media platform effectively, and some of these are premium software. You should try to invest in these social media tools if you can; you'll boost your social media marketing campaigns and measure your improvements effectively.

Step 7: *Analyze Your Integrated Social Media Campaigns* — The next step in ensuring that you have successful social media campaigns is analyzing your effort in promoting your brand. In all honesty, you can never get it right at all time with social media marketing, and you always need to stay up-to-date with the frequent changes in the industry.

There are always new changes that come up in social media platforms that you need to tweak into your social media marketing. You need to stay on top of the latest trends to ensure your success.

There is no perfect social media marketing plan, and everyone has to make changes once in a while to make their plans more effective. By using analytical tools that are available on most social media platforms, you can analyze how your campaigns have been going and understand the changes you can make to make your plan more effective. With these tools, you can find out which posts have more engagement and responses, and which of these posts lead to an increase in sales and leads. You can also find information like how much time your audience spends reading or looking at your content, the location of the people who visited your platforms the most, and the age range of the people who frequent your platforms.

This information is beneficial in analyzing how your campaign is faring and determining what you need to change to help your social media campaign perform better. You can understand what your audience prefers by knowing which posts have more engagement, and you can replicate similar patterns to generate a more significant positive response from your future content.

When you determine the age range of the people who visit your platform, and you can tweak your content to engage these people more, and the process increases responsiveness on your platform.

The information and data from these analytical tools have proven to be useful in improving social media marketing strategies. You should try to include them in your plan, especially as one of the final steps in developing your marketing campaigns.

Social media marketing is a continuous process, and you should always keep an eye out for changes that are made to these platforms. You should make use of these changes to improve your social media marketing and try to use all of the tools available to you, both free and premium, to enhance your marketing campaign.

Your Quick Start Action Step:

Here are some quick start action steps you need to take for your social media marketing campaigns:

1. *Know your audience and the social media platforms on which you can find them. Research your brand and its preferred audience by studying the competition.*
2. *Choose the suitable social media platforms and study how to use them effectively.*
3. *Study the suitable content that will help your social media marketing campaign grow and succeed.*
4. *Learn more about how to use social media analytical tools to analyze your campaigns and find ways to improve.*
5. *Continue the process and keep studying ways to improve.*

Chapter 12: Measuring Your Social Media Marketing Progress with Metrics

Chapter 12: Measuring Your Social Media Marketing Progress with Metrics

12.1 Reviewing Your Progress

In the previous chapter, we discussed steps on how to start and get the most out of your social media campaigns. Each step will help and guide you in promoting your brand and increasing sales while staying ahead of the competition.

The steps mentioned in the previous chapter were designed to take your social media marketing campaign through each step to attain the given objectives of the social media campaign. As each process leads to the next, we saw that we understood our audience, and then learning what content to pass to our audience, before finally making use of the social media tools available to refine and better our plans.

In this chapter, we are going to look at how reviewing our progress and customers' feedback can help our efforts in our social media marketing. We have to use what we have gathered from reviewing our progress and customer feedback and implement them in our plan to make the procedure more effective.

Metrics are used to measure how an audience is engaged in a social media platform and the rate of that engagement.

With useful analyses using these metrics, you'll know how to tweak social media marketing to get much better results in following your objectives. Now, we are going look at some of the useful metrics we can use to measure the success of our social media campaigns, and how we can use them to do better in our campaigns and get closer to our objectives:

- *The Growth of Your Followers* — Keeping track of the number of followers you have both before and during the campaign is one way to measure your progress. This metric helps you determine if you are successful with your campaign; a steady increase in followers shows that you are doing well. When there is no positive progress in the number of followers, or there is a decrease in your number of followers, you may have to reconsider your marketing approach. You should then check if you are targeting the right people with the right content.

- *The number of Likes and Comments on Your Content* — You can also use the metrics of likes and comments on your content to determine if you are engaging your targeted audience with the right content. You can use this metric to determine if the content that you are posting is really what your audience desires. If they like the content, the likes and shares will increase, and there will be more engagement on your profile. You should reconsider the content of your posts if there is less engagement, and do more research to determine what your audience is looking for in your content.

- *Your Mentions* — You'll know how often people are talking about you by tracking your mentions on these platforms. You can also determine the audience reaction by whether the comments are positive or negative. From these metrics, you can learn how to use this information to improve your social media campaigns further. If you find out that the reactions are not favorable, you can find a way to manage the situation and help turn things around. An increase in mentions shows that you are increasing awareness about your platform, and encouraging the process you are using to market your brand on this platform.

- *Knowledge of Your Target Demographic* — Social media tools can help you gauge the demographics of your social media plan and determine how to use your content. The demographics can also help you plan your social media advertising campaigns. If demographics show that more women are visiting your platform, then you should focus more on reaching out to women with your resources to meet your objectives. With this information, you can plan your content to target a specific audience and increase engagement and sales.

- *The Reach of Your Content* — The reach of your content can determine the number of people that have come across your content, as well as how far your content reaches. This measures both targeted audiences and shares on various platforms. It is a way to determine how far your content has gone and determines responsiveness and awareness in regards to your content. It can show that your content is interesting and useful enough to be shared among your followers, and those who don't follow you yet, as well.

These are some of the tools that you can use to measure your metrics. These will help you analyze your platform and determine what changes to make to help you grow and attain your objectives.

12.2 Importance of Using Metrics and Tracking Your Progress

Unfortunately, many people do not have the time to track their social media marketing campaigns. They spend most of their time providing content, and little to no time checking their progress and metrics.

Here, we'll highlight the importance of tracking your progress and using metrics to measure your success:

- *You Get to Know Your Audience* — You research your targeted viewers before you start your social media campaigns, and tracking your progress during this campaign will determine the demographic and audiences viewing your posts. It is only through this analysis that you can truly decide which audiences are interested in your posts and content. This information gained through using metrics is used to tweak your posts and content further to reach out even more to these audiences.

- *Spend Fewer Resources in Reaching Your Target Audience* — Going on a wild goose chase on social media platforms is not encouraging, and will require you to spend more resources. After all that, you still might not end up reaching your target audience. If you track the progress of your social media marketing, you can determine your target audience, who is interested in your brand, and what works for you as you funnel your resources to those avenues and reduce expenses. Use this metric to determine what does and doesn't work, and do away with anything ineffective.

- *Increase Awareness and Leads* — There is no better way to increase awareness and leads to your brand than by checking your progress. When you do this, you will know which content and campaigns had higher response and increased sales. With this knowledge, you can promote those posts more and engage even more people.

- *Determine What Is Effective* — Using metrics to monitor your progress helps you determine what is and is not working. You'll know which posts generate the most response through likes, shares, and total comments. You can determine what is not working and do away with those strategies. With this knowledge, you can focus on what is working and draw closer to your objectives. You will ultimately spend more time on successful ventures and become more productive.

- *Increase Engagement on Your Platform* — Social media analytic tools can show the number of comments there is on a particular post, and you can use this to your advantage.

When you notice that some topics are more engaging than others, and there are more comments on that content, you should continue to promote that content to your audience. This action would lead to increase engagement and response on your platform while you continue to initiate more interesting conversations.

12.3 How to Track Social Media Marketing Progress with Metrics

You have started your social media marketing campaign, and you have started reaching out to your target audience as you grow your brand. So much data is flying around as you begin to analyze how your campaign is performing.

Through all of this, the question we are going to answer now is how to track social media marketing progress through metrics. You can track your progress in several different ways:

1. *Number of Followers* — Your total number of followers will determine whether you are doing a good job or a bad job in your marketing campaign. If you have the same amount of

followers as you had when you started the campaign, then you have not made any changes, either positive or negative. A positive change will show that your followers have increased since the start of the campaign while losing followers would be a negative result. Always keep an eye on the number of followers you have and how that number changes over time. When possible, determine what causes those changes.

2. *Mentions on These Platforms* — Mentions on social media are a great way to show how much response you've had to your campaign. With mentions, you can determine what people are saying about your brand, and the more mentions you have, the more the awareness for your brand is growing. You can engage with your audience directly when you get notified of their mentions, and you'll earn more trust with your audience.

3. *Audience Reaction to Your Campaign* — The number of mentions is essential, but it is also important to know what people are saying, and how they feel about your brand. You can let

positive comments build up on their own. However, you should respond to negative comments constructively. Whenever you get mentioned, and you notice it is a negative comment, approach the commenter tactfully and respectfully as you get them to explain why they reacted that way. In these cases, you should encourage a direct and constructive conversation to find a solution to whatever issue they have with your brand. With negative comments or sentiments, try to solve the problem to prevent damage to your brand's reputation.

4. *Interactions with Influencers* — There are many influencers on social media platforms, and getting an influencer to promote your brand is a big deal. An influencer will do more to promote your brand when they endorse your product. However, when you become a topic of discussion among influencers in the industry, then your brand is becoming one of the most trusted in the industry. This interaction is another way of measuring your progress on social media platforms: influencers start

talking about you without expecting any favors in return.

5. *Increase in Leads to Your Website from Social Media Platforms* — You can track the number of visitors coming to your website, and where they are coming from. When there is an increase in the number of people from your social media platforms visiting your site, then you have made an enormous impact. This finding shows that your audience finds your content attractive on social media, so they visit your website for more.

6. *Increase in Conversion Rate* — Money is a huge determining factor in the success of efforts from social media marketing. This aspect is a significant metric used to measure a business's success in social media marketing. When there is a noticeable increase in return on investment (ROI) of the brand during the social media campaign, this is considered a positive sign or positive result. This can also be classified as an increase in conversion rate with an increase in awareness due to the marketing campaign.

Your Quick Start Action Step:

We can keep track of the data and information right from the start as we study the gradual process of the campaign and make a note of its progress. However, this is the preliminary stage, and any records taken during this period may be for a quick analysis.

If you want an analysis that you can use to check on the metrics or steps in determining the progress, then you must wait awhile. You have to give some time for your marketing campaign to take effect, so you can have good results to work with when using the analytic tools available.

Let the campaign run for two or three months before taking the data and analyzing it effectively. Here are some quick steps to take to record your social media marketing progress:

1. *Write down your number of followers, your sales volume, and other parameters that you can use to gauge your progress at the start of your social media marketing efforts.*
2. *Embark on rigorous social media marketing using the ideas and strategies you have learned in this book.*

3. *Revisit your notes and write down the number of followers, sales volume, reposts, comments, and reshares. Compare that number with what you recorded at the start of your social media campaign.*

4. *Keep recording these numbers monthly, starting from the third month of your social media marketing campaign, and make a note of the increase. That increase is a measure of the success of your social media marketing efforts.*

Bonus Chapter: Advanced Strategies to Increase Your Following on Social Media

Bonus Chapter: Advanced Strategies to Increase Your Following on Social Media

Growing your social media following is not magic or rocket science. Here are some strategies to adopt in order to increase your social media audience significantly. The strategies discussed in this section will target your Facebook, Twitter, YouTube, and Instagram followers.

Facebook

Step 1: Run Facebook Ads

You no longer need to be told that you need a Facebook account to run Facebook ads. Upon creating your Facebook page, running paid Facebook ads like "Engagement Ads" will help push your business to many followers, increase your visibility, and encourage many to explore your page.

Step 2: Invite People to Like Your Page

Another good option, especially for those with

thousands of friends on Facebook, is to invite them to like your page individually. This effort will make it easier to get across to all friends and family, and they can also help by inviting their friends. Ensure you keep track of the number of people you invite at a time to prevent being temporarily blocked.

Step 3: Create Visual Content

If you want to capture your followers' attention, use visual content. When your followers know that they will always find funny memes, useful video, relatable quotes, and other informative visual content on your page, they will be more inclined to follow you. Such content helps improve your social media engagement, and when it goes viral, there is no limit to what you can achieve.

Step 4: Host Giveaways

If you need more likes, more followers, and a more dedicated and active audience, then giveaways are the key. Everyone loves freebies, so when you offer them gifts from time to time for being active, they will stay active and will also invite others to enjoy the benefits.

Step 5: Try Facebook Live

The easiest way to go viral and improve your Facebook engagement is through Facebook live videos. Have you added new products? Do you offer new services? Are you trying to engage your followers? Then this is the best option for you.

Twitter

Step 1: Post great content

Twitter is all about what you post. Lousy tweets won't earn you quality followers. So, if you want to improve your twitter response, it is best to start by posting relevant and high-quality content that will encourage many to explore all that you offer. The more quality content you deliver, the more followers you'll get.

Step 2: Use Hashtags

Every minute of every hour of every day, there are new trending hashtags on Twitter. If you stay relevant and reach a quality audience, it is best to follow and tweet using the trending hashtags. Tweets delivered with the most relevant and trending hashtags will motivate users to follow you.

Step 3: Promote Your Tweet

After preparing an awesome tweet, you need to get that tweet to your active followers. If other methods you've used have failed to deliver, your next option is to promote your tweet. Promoting your tweet will help push your services to a larger audience, whether they are your followers or not.

Step 4: Engage with Others on Twitter

Twitter is all about engaging with other users. So, if you want to reach a larger audience, it is best to interact with them regularly. This interaction may include retweeting their tweets, liking their posts, and commenting on useful tweets. Before you know it, your following will drastically increase.

YouTube

Step 1: Don't Hack; Promote Your Videos

If you go online to search for a free hack on how to improve your YouTube subscriber base, you are planting a tree that will be fruitless. Build a solid plan to promote your YouTube channel. This process can start with manual tasks like outsourcing subscribers individually. Upon accomplishing this, you're sure to have more active subscribers.

Step 2: Be Consistent with Your Delivery

If your channel is active for a while, you need to deliver a lot of content consistently. Subscribers expect you to post; when they realize that you are not providing enough useful content, they'll end up unsubscribing from your channel. However, if your relevant videos keep popping up when they search online, your account will keep growing. Building a publishing schedule will improve the size of your audience.

Step 3: Convert Searchers to Subscribers with Playlist

Acquiring a first-time viewer is not an easy task. You need relevant keywords to help people see your videos, so if they see it, at least you have tried. But it doesn't end there. Is your video captivating and relevant enough to turn first-time viewers into subscribers? A playlist is an option to help keep subscribers for your channel. With a playlist, you can boost your content consumption and watch time. Create tracks of content for new users, task-oriented viewers, and topic-focused viewers. This approach will help turn your viewers into subscribers.

Step 4: Promote Your Channel on Other Sites

Do you have other social media accounts? Do you offer your products on an e-commerce site? If you do, then a great way of improving your following is by promoting your channel on these platforms. You can make use of Facebook groups, add a mention in Amazon reviews, or share your channel link on social media. This strategy is excellent for growing your audience.

Instagram

Step 1: Use Hashtags Effectively

The best way to promote your posts is through the use of hashtags. In situations where you develop a unique hashtag for your industry, make sure you promote it by printing in on your receipts and ads. When adding captions to your post, use relevant, quality hashtags to capture attention.

Step 2: Participate in Popular Conversation

If you make it big on Instagram, you need to be active and outgoing. Participate in conversations regularly, and remember to leave your footprint on every comment you drop. Many will be interested in knowing what you offer.

Step 3: Explore Instagram Stories

Instagram stories have been around for a while now, and many Instagram users have been making use of them. You too can reap the reward of a broad audience if you explore this option. Posting relevant content will help turn viewers into active subscribers for your service.

Step 4: Promote Your Posts

The best way to reach a larger and more unique audience is through the use of sponsored posts on Instagram. Paying Instagram to help broadcast your posts to subscribers and non-subscribers guarantees that many people will hear about your service. Remember, the more relevant the sponsored post is, the more efficient it will be in getting you more followers.

The strategies discussed above are guaranteed to help you gain more followers. Also, they will help you retain your following, as long as you consistently follow the approach. Your business is not meant to sit off on the sidelines.

It should be discovered by others who will find value in your products and services, and your social media presence will play an active part in that.

Bonus Sneak Peek

"Content Marketing"

I want to share with you a Sneak Peek into another book of mine that I think you will enjoy.

The book is called "Content Marketing" and it's about marketing your products and services using compelling content. Enjoy this free chapter!

Chapter 7: Content Marketing Strategies

7.1 Content Marketing Strategy

For both the successful business as well for the new company, the content marketing strategy is crucial. When you plan, create, and post your content on different online platforms, that content marketing is called strategic content marketing. The process of taking the content and using a strategic plan so that it eventually leads to a sale is called a content marketing strategy. This strategy is evaluated at every platform, including blogs, social media, websites, and more. Why do you need a solid content marketing strategy?

The answer is to build a business reputation and to achieve business goals.

As marketing costs and ad costs to use platforms such as Google, Facebook Marketing or even Instagram continue to go up, approaches like content marketing and SEO become ever more critical because it doesn't cost any money after that piece of content has been created--it just keeps going forever and ever.

Content marketing is utilizing any type of content, whether that be something physical or digital, and turning it into a valuable, informational or entertaining asset, or a combination of all of the above: infotainment. You take your content and turn it into something that your potential audience will use and find practical. This way, they can decide what the content offers them and use it in their day-to-day lives, and it provides value to their day.

Characteristics of a Perfect Content Marketing Strategy:

- Identify your best platforms. Where are your customers spending their time online? Are they on Facebook, are they on Instagram? Are they looking at Medium, are they on YouTube, are they coming to your blog? Think about that and identify the best platforms for reaching your audience. Your business may be better suited to marketing content on some platforms than others, and that is perfectly okay. Narrow your focus to the platforms where your customers are. Give some thought to which platforms are best targeted when it comes to the product or service you offer and get yourself on there, ready to connect with customers.

- Build your content library. Do a lot of research and collect content upfront. There are a variety of different ways to do that, and a variety of different types of content. Give some thought to the different types of content. Let's take a few examples. One type of content is customer reviews. You can capture all these customer reviews and build out a stockpile of this type of content that you can trickle out on social media over time, or on all your different content sources and platforms. Another example would be infographics or stats. Do you have specific infographics or stats for your industry? These don't need to be graphics and statistics that you've created yourself; these could be the stats and infographics generated by other sources but *are related to your business*. You can collect a big library of these statistics or infographics that would be interesting and valuable to your followers to see (make sure you cite those sources!). You can then later use that data to create some of your own design assets. Some other examples would be finding quotes--industry-specific quotes or quotes that you have come up with yourself--and build out an inventory for those. Videos are a type of content, as are images--photos of your company, pictures of your products. If you build out this idea library, adding on all these different content types and stockpiling these out in advance, you will save a ton of time moving forward when you need content "in the now" to post under your social media platforms.

- Create your cadence. What are you posting, what types of content are you providing to your audience every day? Or every week? When you are building your content library, you'll have all these different ideas and all these different types of content that you want to provide. Once you do that, you'll be able to visualize what you want to post. So as an example, you may wish to post a quote in the morning, and then post a stat in the afternoon, and possibly post a video in the evening. But you need to have a cadence, so there's something of a rhythm to your social media posts. Whether it's a daily rhythm or a weekly rhythm, you have that cadence--that thought that you've put into it in advance so that you know what type of content you need for the week or for the day. If you have your idea library, it is going to make it much easier to fall into this cadence than if you were trying to post useful content off the top of your head as opposed to thinking about that at that very moment. So give some thought to what type of cadence would be appropriate for your business and what would drive value to your viewers.

- Develop a posting schedule. Once you have your content library built up and you've considered the type of cadence that would be appropriate for your business and provide value to your customers, you need a regular schedule for making your content marketing strategy into a tangible reality. What does your schedule look like? Will you be posting one time a day, three times a day, five times a day? Under which platforms will you be posting content? Do you need to post multiple content types to various platforms? We would recommend posting between one and three times a day on each platform you decide to use for your content marketing. The three times per day approach is beneficial to you because you could be reaching your audience when they wake up, when they eat lunch, and when they go to bed. Studies show that this is when people look at content most often. If you schedule three types of content to post during those particular times of the day, that will be perfect. And then figure out the cadence: Are you posting quotes in the morning, videos in the afternoon, that kind of thing? Once you've made that happen, it will be time to develop your schedule template. When you do this, think in terms of building a schedule template for the week, that way you can use your template each week as a guide, and you can populate the template with the content for your posts during the week.

- Document as you go. The idea library is fantastic for just pre-populating all this content so you hardly even have to think about it. When you add in the cadence and the schedule, you have posts that are ready to go, scheduled and dialed in. But aside from that, you also need to document as you go. So as cool things happen, you come across things, you take pictures of stuff, you do some live videos of yourself, so document as you go, and that way you can post this stuff in real time as it occurs. You can layer that in on top of your pre-fabricated, pre-scheduled content. You can also look at what works, what causes click-throughs and engagement, and what doesn't. This way, you can document what content works and what may need to be reshaped or pulled altogether.

- Be efficient. Use a tool like Hootsuite, which is a tool that lets you pre-schedule your posts, so they send out at the correct times. It also contains some metrics in there that you can use from a results perspective, to get a better look at how you're doing. The system also allows you to do some engagement, which is nice because it will enable you to streamline a lot of these activities that would otherwise be done by hand, one by one, which can get time-consuming--and time is money. You can pre-schedule things to post to various social media platforms using one tool like Hootsuite to do all of this in one place.

- Engagement. You don't want to necessarily just be pushing content all the time. With social media marketing, in particular, you want to be *social*, so you want to like, comment, follow other people, and engage with the community. Be involved. So don't just post your content, actually be an active engager of *other* content. This action is going to help you increase your brand awareness, and mainly grow your followers over time, and it will do so much more quickly than if you're exclusively pushing your own content.

- Add value. Don't just post for the sake of merely posting. Make sure that every post delivers some value to your followers. Otherwise, they'll stop following you and stop engaging with you--and stop buying from you. Share-worthy content plus share-worthy design, plus engagement, equals success. And the key to all of that is delivering value, every time.

- Track your results and make adjustments accordingly. If you see that you've gotten more engagement, more likes, more sharing, of your posts that are made in the evening, consider doing more posts in the evening, or adjust the times that your posts are going live. In another example, if you see a particular type of post that you're doing, maybe it's one where you're highlighting different stats in your industry, and you see that this one has a lot of engagement, consider doing some more of those and see if you continue to build more engagement when you do. If another post, like your customer reviews, isn't doing as well, consider doing fewer of those. So, look at your data, start to understand what your followers want to see, and give them more of what they like. It's common sense, but it's also effective marketing.

- Find some social media role models. Find some role models in your industry, who you think are doing a great job on social media, who are delivering content value to you. Then, you can do a bit of reverse engineering, and give some thought to how you can use some of those ideas as inspiration for yourself. This can help guide you in the type of content and strategy that you can successfully implement for *your* brand.

- Stay relevant. Make sure that you're connected to the subject matter for your social media content and your brand. People who are following you for advice and information on, say, quality dance clothes, don't really care what you did this weekend when you went kayaking or in seeing pictures of your dog;

they're not so interested in that. What they *are* interested in, though, is dance apparel. If that's your niche and your industry, stay within that wheelhouse. Talk about that, be an expert on that, add value to that, and *that* will be what increases your following.

- Brand your social media platforms. Make sure they're professionally designed, streamlined and consistent, that you have good profile pictures, and that you populate all the areas of content. The about us, your website links, your other social links, videos, don't ignore a single populated field. Because what's going to happen is people who are following you, and like your content, at some point, they're going to want to move forward with your brand.-- possibly to become a customer. When that happens, you want them to be able to do that right from your social platform, very quickly. You want to be accessible so that people will be able to click through to your website, see your call to action, and take that next step. By taking the time to brand those social media platforms, you have that laid in so that it's a smooth conversion funnel for your followers.

- Invest in a paid advertisement. Although providing content and engaging with followers (and following relevant others) are compelling from an organic perspective, paid advertisement can take things to the next level and get you some serious sales boosts. Doing some campaigns, spending some money boosting your post, gets it out in front of more people than you would be able to do organically alone. Do some retargeting campaigns, and some other things on the paid side, to supercharge your growth on the social side.

- Don't stop doing it. Keep focusing on your content strategy. So many times, we see good content start coming out from a brand, and then it stops. Poof. What that means is the content provider just stopped investing time in it. They ended spending on online resources. You need to make sure you stay consistent. You're not going see tremendous growth overnight. But if you continually post content and keep an eye on your content strategy and engage with your followers, you're going to go from 100 followers to 1,000 eventually after several months, to 2,000, and three years from now it could be hundreds of thousands. The question is: Did you stick with it or not? Because the growth is there, it's just something you need to keep working on and continue optimizing. So if you do not have time to invest in it yourself, hire somebody, or hire another company to do it for you, but make sure that you're investing in doing it to get results.

How a content marketing strategy works:

1. The first step to do is to create your goals and objectives. Content flow planning is just any kind of planning involved in the creation and implementation of your content. I find it is useful because it allows you to be able to draw arrows to things and line things up in a diagram. Goals and objectives should be considered: Are you trying to drive leads with your content, are you trying to you know build sales for your content, are you just trying to inform your audience with your content?

2. Digital marketing agencies can help to target

specific keywords. If you want to start ranking higher, you need to get the content that you want to rank at number one on Google or YouTube, and it's just up to what stage you're at in the funnel. Create a high-level strategy using specific keywords when creating content. Searching keywords for content marketing is like creating a sub-strategy. This sub-strategy focuses on main sets of keywords and gives you an idea of how to move forward with content creation.

3. Next, create your buyer personas. And if you don't have an idea who your buyer personas are, you can do some research to figure them out. These are the same people who are going to be engaging with your content. Review your objectives and think of demographics. For example, males between the ages of 18 to 35 who are entrepreneurs. If you spread this out a little bit so you get little room for entrepreneurs would be for marketers, college dropouts, or people never went to college, people who want total personal control over their careers. Whatever characteristics your buyers have--that's what you want to lay out, because this helps you determine what you need to focus on to get this type of content to that person.

4. Another step you need to take is to get your content audited. The content audit is an in-depth analysis where you can see all keywords and their rankings. The content audit enables you to put all of this information together to figure out the best way to reach customers. To do this, you can use a tool called Google Search Console, and it shows you all of the traffic that your content receives. It's able to show you all of your keywords and their specific rank on the Google search engine. The only way you can do a content audit is if you have content currently, so if you are just beginning your content marketing journey, you can't perform a content audit yet. However, even new businesses have the option of analyzing your *competitor's* content. Look at the content of the competition. See how people engage and react to that kind of content.

5. Having a content management system can save you from a future headache. You can create, schedule, and post your content directly from a content management system. There are many reliable CMS in the market, like WordPress, HubSpot, Hootsuite, and more.

6. After the content audit, you know where you stand currently and what keywords might be good for targeting. The next thing to do is get into the keyword research phase. Keyword research can be done with several tools like Google Keyword Planner--keywords everywhere. Another great tool is Ubersuggest. You'll start with your high-level keywords: for example, "marketing agency." Doing so will give you a bunch of suggestions that can be used. In Google Keyword Planner, you go to the planner and click find "new keywords." To do this, you do have to have an ad manager account. Make sure you have that set up first, and then you can click to get started. Then it's going to start showing you the keywords as well as the competition. You need to opt to target lower competition with high search volume keywords. Then you'll need to create an Excel spreadsheet to keep a record of these keywords. It shows the keyword list, and their volume and the competition for that particular keyword. Next up is Google Trends. If you know your keywords but you're stumped on what to choose first then this tool can be your guide. Using it tells how relevant a keyword is over time. It shows the searches according to their geographical area,

allowing you to choose the best-trending keywords from your list.

7. The next step in content marketing is to prioritize the content. After collecting the keywords to create content, you can create a plan to use specific keywords for a specific time. The easier to target will be used first and then the rest. You can also create a schedule to publish content on a month-to-month basis. So prioritize your topics make sure that everything makes sense. You need to pick a niche in the beginning and stick with that niche and become the expert.

8. Finally, you need to set your content calendar. Once you prioritize your topics and your keywords, then you need to create article topics based on those keywords. Creating content off-the-cuff is not a great strategy, but creating consistent and engaging content is the most promising way to attract customers. On the other hand, a content calendar also reduces the load of content creation as well as it can help you in A/B testing. It's just making sure that you're doing everything and planning everything to be well-executed. If you're not taking these steps, it's going to

be difficult to create a content marketing plan that achieves success. Once you have the content marketing plan in place for the first 30 to 45 days, you can create a campaign-planning calendar, where you can go in and add topics for the future.

7.2 Why Content Marketing Strategy Is Important

Why is content marketing strategy so important for your business?

The following are some points that show the importance of content marketing strategy:

• You are probably already aware of how important it is to follow up with a person you have personally approached to convert them from a lead to a paying customer. Using pushy sales tactics and badgering with weekly follow-ups could lead to pushing them away rather than converting them. However, what if you deliver content to them that helped to educate them on the services or products you offer that interest them?

• By effectively utilizing content marketing strategy, you start adding value, and you build trust. This plan is going to make you stand out from your competition and have a positive impact on your conversion rate because you will get more organic visitors to your website.

• Content marketing strategy gives you free and organic traffic you don't have to pay for. You do pay for the content that you put up on your website (blogs, videos, etc.) upfront. But once you start ranking for that content, if somebody sees your listing in the SERPs and they click on that organic result, then you're not paying for that traffic. Applying this strategy adds massive value to your website and will start generating new leads and sales 24/7.

• A solid strategy will help you to address buyer objections. By surveying your customers and prospects, you will conclude what their complaints or needs are. Once you understand these things, then you should create content centered around that. You can then use that in your email follow-ups, blog posts, videos, and even in eBooks. Anything that can answer those buyer objections will help increase your conversion rates.

• You can use concepts for lead generation. For

example, any paid ads that you're running, you can use those as free give away. To create a mini-eBook or a whitepaper or a checklist, something of value that helps educate your customers on whatever you do. That's a freebie, but it doesn't have to be a loss. You can give this content away for free, and the customer provides their name and their email address to you, which gives you a potential customer email list, and you can start dripping them with content.

• Creating a content strategy helps you get a series of new and recurring visitors, which you would not have otherwise had access to. By creating a content marketing strategy, you can convert leads to customers.

• A perfect content marketing strategy helps you to retarget your customers. For example, when somebody visits your site but doesn't contact you, so you don't have their email, and you don't know their information, but you did pixel them. Through looking at the tracking pixel, you will know which product they're interested in. Assessing this can help you retarget them with ads, and those ads can provide answers to those buyer objections. They might have to click to that ad, which could be a free download of some content and this would get them to your email list and then convert them from a lead to a customer. Thus, a perfect content marketing strategy is the key to your business goals, whether it is being carried out via a website or on social media.

To learn more about "Content Marketing" and how it can help you create great Social Media content, look for "Content Marketing: Proven Strategies to Attract an Engaged Audience Online with Great Content and Social Media to Win More Customers, Build your Brand and Boost your Business" by Gavin Turner on Amazon.com.

Conclusion

Through social media marketing, you can reach more people than with any other form of marketing. What is the implication of this? There is no limit to the magic of this marketing strategy. When I embraced this effective method of marketing, my business moved far ahead of those of my competitors. It never remained the same. I was surprised when I considered my achievement within a year of launching my social markcting campaign. I would never have imagined that I could make such a profit in such a short span of time!

The same strategies that turned my business around have been simplified in the pages of this guide book. We started by explaining the importance and relevance of social media in your industry. This book contains a step-by-step guide on how to becomes successful with your social media marketing campaign. It explains, in detail, how you can attract the attention of the right people who will ultimately become your clients and customers. Not only that, it describes how you can incorporate your business goals with your social media accounts. Of course, you need the right mindset to succeed in this approach, which this book has outlined extensively.

By now, you know what it takes to promote your business on social media platforms like Facebook, Instagram, YouTube, and Twitter. This book has also provided you with a way of gauging the success of your social media marketing efforts, so you can know if your marketing efforts are yielding fruit, or if you have to re-strategize.

On a final note, the results of social media marketing are incredible, and there is no limit to the benefits of this strategy. With its wider reach, it can help your business go global, increase your customer base, and, of course, boost your sales. With this book in your hands, no business goal is unachievable with the help of social media marketing. Good luck!

Leave a Review

Finally, if you enjoyed this book, I'd appreciate it if you leave your honest feedback. You can do so by visiting the book's page on Amazon.com.

References

23 Ideas for Marketers Wondering What to Post on Instagram. (n.d.). Retrieved from https://unmetric.com/resources/things-to-post-on-instagram

7 Steps for an Effective Social Media Marketing Plan. (2018, July 29). Retrieved from https://ducttapemarketing.com/social-media-marketing-plan/

Agius, A. (2016, November 07). 10 Metrics to Track for Social Media Success. Retrieved from https://www.socialmediaexaminer.com/10-metrics-to-track-for-social-media-success/

Barnhart. (2019, May 01). How to build your social media marketing strategy for 2019. Retrieved from https://sproutsocial.com/insights/social-media-marketing-strategy/

Campbell, C. (2019, January 04). Instagram Ads: How to Advertise on Instagram in 2019. Retrieved from https://www.shopify.com/blog/instagram-ads

Collins, J. (2019, April 26). YouTube 101: What Beginners Need to Know About Using YouTube. Retrieved from https://www.lifewire.com/youtube-101-3481847

Cuninghame, C. (2019, February 19). How to write tweets that go viral! (well, almost viral). Retrieved from https://copywritematters.com/how-to-write-tweets/

Detisch, A. (n.d.). 161 Creative YouTube Video Ideas to Try. Retrieved from https://www.google.com/amp/s/www.studiobinder.com/blog/creative-youtube-video-ideas-list/amp/?espv=1

Gordon, K. (n.d.). Topic: Social Media Statistics. Retrieved from https://www.statista.com/topics/1164/social-networks/

Hainla, L. (2018, July 5). 21 Social Media Marketing Statistics You Need to Know in 2019. Retrieved from https://www.dreamgrow.com/21-social-media-marketing-statistics/

Hausman, A. (2016, September 08). 16 Differences

Between Traditional Media and Social Networking.
Retrieved   from
https://www.hausmanmarketingletter.com/16-
differences-between-social-media-and-traditional-
media/

Hendricks, D. (2013, May 06). Complete History of
Social Media: Then and Now. Retrieved from
https://smallbiztrends.com/2013/05/the-complete-
history-of-social-media-infographic.html

Lozano, D. (2016, August 25). 5 Under-Used Twitter
Features That Can Help Your Business Stand Out
Online.   Retrieved   from
https://www.socialmediatoday.com/social-
networks/5-under-used-twitter-features-can-help-
your-business-stand-out-online

Nations, D. (2019, March 29). What Is Facebook?
Here's What You Should Know. Retrieved from
https://www.lifewire.com/what-is-facebook-3486391

Newberry, C. (2018, August 20). How to Use Twitter
Ads: The Complete Guide for Marketers. Retrieved
from https://blog.hootsuite.com/twitter-ads/

Rouse, M. (n.d.). What is Twitter? - Definition from

WhatIs.com. Retrieved from https://whatis.techtarget.com/definition/Twitter

Rouse, M. (n.d.). What is Instagram? - Definition from WhatIs.com. Retrieved from https://searchcio.techtarget.com/definition/Instagra m

Shane, D. (2017, April 26). The 7 Mindset Shifts Needed for Successful Social Media Marketing. Retrieved from https://medium.com/the-mission/the-7-mindset-shifts-needed-for-successful-social-media-marketing-96b614bde193

Why is Content So Important in Social Media Marketing? (n.d.). Retrieved from https://www.godotmedia.com/importance-of-content-social-media-marketing/

Zhou, W. (2016, August 31). 7 New YouTube Features and How Marketers Can Leverage Them. Retrieved from https://www.techwyse.com/blog/social-media-marketing/youtube-features/amp/

Made in the USA
Columbia, SC
29 September 2019